T3-BEE-988

# Reflections in Communication

## An Interdisciplinary Approach

Alusine M. Kanu

UNIVERSITY PRESS OF AMERICA, ® INC.
*Lanham • Boulder • New York • Toronto • Plymouth, UK*

**Copyright © 2009 by**
**University Press of America,® Inc.**
4501 Forbes Boulevard
Suite 200
Lanham, Maryland 20706
UPA Acquisitions Department (301) 459-3366

Estover Road
Plymouth PL6 7PY
United Kingdom

All rights reserved
Printed in the United States of America
British Library Cataloging in Publication Information Available

Library of Congress Control Number: 2008934820
ISBN-13: 978-0-7618-4162-3 (paperback : alk. paper)
ISBN-10: 0-7618-4162-8 (paperback : alk. paper)
eISBN-13: 978-0-7618-4186-9
eISBN-10: 0-7618-4186-5

∞™ The paper used in this publication meets the minimum
requirements of American National Standard for Information
Sciences—Permanence of Paper for Printed Library Materials,
ANSI Z39.48—1992

# Contents

# Acknowledgments

I would like to acknowledge the Liberal Arts Department of Northern Virginia Community College, and the valuable staff of George Mason University for their encouragement in my study of Communication, with concentration in Speech Communication Education and Organization. I would also like to thank my immediate family, Geraldine, Daniel, Hawanatu, and my grandchildren Paul and Esther. I am a native of Sierra Leone, West Africa and would like to thank my Father, Mr. Amadu M. Kanu for inspiration, mother, Saffie Kamara for caring, and my immediate and distant relatives both in the United States and in Sierra Leone, West Africa. This text is also an attribution of friendship to Margaret Prudham, Daniel Rainey, Stephanie Shaffer, Gail Kehlewell, and the many Global citizens that made my efforts worthwhile, and God's guidance.

# Introduction

## *Reflections, Learning is the Eye of the Mind*

### Thomas Drake

It is a pleasure to introduce *Reflections in Communication*. The purpose of this material is that it brings together a number of pieces towards earning my doctorate in Speech Communication at George Mason University in Fairfax VA. In addition, I have had extensive experiences in teaching for courses in speech communication for 25 years. I teach, or have taught, Introduction to Speech Communication, Interpersonal Communication, Small Group Communication, Public Speaking, Intercultural Communication, and Organizational Communication. I have taught, or teach, at Northern Virginia Community College in Annandale VA, George Mason University in Fairfax VA, Towson University in Baltimore MD, Coppin State College in Baltimore MD, and at Millersville University in Pennsylvania.

The material for this text is for students in a hybrid course in Speech Communication, either labeled Introduction to Speech Communication or Fundamentals of Speech Communication. The audience, therefore, is students enrolled in basic Communication courses or for anyone who might be interested in learning about communication.

Many commentators will agree that the level of intellectual aspiration is not very imposing. They are always for localizing the truth, for assuring the answers to the basic questions about life and answering them in a casual, pragmatic and applicable matter.

The goal is to stage an understanding of the fundamental principles of Communication as they apply in a wide variety of situations. It might be used for people who need an understanding of the theories and concepts of life-long communication skills. It is dramatically different because it employs an experiential, critical and interdisciplinary approach to the field of Communication. It uses a variety of classroom structures. The basic principles and concepts that will be covered in this text are: The elements of Communication, three views of human nature, definition and types of Communication, models of communication, self-concept, perception, verbal, nonverbal, listening, interviewing, interpersonal communication, small group communication, public speaking, intercultural communication, and speaking to inform in a free speech society. It involves critical thinking and knowledgeable insights and criticism and will act as a resource for basic communication skills in dealing with varied cultures in our global village.

The study of human communication began about 25,000 years ago when the earth emerged from pre-history and left us with the oldest surviving records of human communication, the cave painting and figures. That story continues through the development of language writing, printing, and the mass media, and ways of exchanging and using information that have made the recent centuries of human communication as distinctive as culture.

This publication, with its major themes, will have stimulating effects in perspectives of self and others in communicating effectively in a democratic society.

This report and analysis describes how various theories of communication interaction are applicable to the general outline of a hybrid basic course. The text focuses on factors of life-long learning and on the contextual nature of an introductory course by reflecting on and showing the usefulness of the fundamental principles of communication as they apply in a variety of situations.

Human communication is the process of making sense out of the world and sharing that sense with others.

The communication interactions and feedback between students relate to such a text in a basic course and is related to the process view of communication. The ideas that we communicate symbols and meaning and that in interacting with others, we engage in symbolic activity make it a process view of communication. What these ideas mean is that students should be concerned with the messages that are exchanged in discussions, and the learning process, as well as with the content of learning. This concern means that basic communication of students should focus on the process of symbols as they relate to learning needs because classroom dynamics make for pleasant, exciting relationships. The basic competency toward communicating is to contact others in ways that affirm their "personhood." That means doing several things, and each chapter that follows is about one or more of those things. It also means that even in a conflict situation, both sender and receiver are choosing to feel as they do, so they both need to own their feelings and be responsible for them. Sharing feelings and listening to the feelings of others is also important. The key is to be aware of your own and the other's personhood and to communicate in ways that manifest and demonstrate affirmation.

This book is an attempt to humanize knowledge by centering the story of speculative thought about human communication.

The curriculum for teaching the basic course will include:

1. The three views of human nature
2. Defining the communication process and its parts:
3. Self Concept
4. Perception
5. Language
6. Nonverbal
7. Listening
8. Culture
9. Interviewing
10. Interpersonal
11. Small Group
12. Public Speaking
13. Freedom of speech

*Chapter One*

# Three Views of Human Nature

## BEHAVIORIST: JOHN WATSON (1919), CLARK HULL (1943), B. F. SKINNER (1974)

Those three names are meant to illustrate authorities on Behaviorism. A basic model of the behaviorists is a learning model analogous to a piece of machinery; there is input, and there is output.

The behaviorist sees humans as basically passive organisms which differ very little from other animals (thus the term organism) and which must be motivated (stimulated by external forces) to perform. Accordingly, we do not have a will of our own and can be adequately explained in terms of stimulus—response behavior.

The behaviorists, who have a response dominated view of humans, are interested primarily in how the environment functions to elicit desired responses from us.

The behaviorists reason that it is unnecessary to speculate about cognitive processes, since one cannot observe them firsthand. Inferences are unscientific, and only that which can be observed and measured is of importance to their model of human nature. Unconscious mental forces are primarily responsible for an individual's behavior.

The behaviorists' model is of an organism conditioned to be in equilibrium with its environment, to behave so as not to disrupt the norms of society.

The behaviorists see a human being as a rational animal, a paradox, since they do not want to be concerned with the mind. Our rational behavior, as opposed to the emotional, stems from the imprinting in our minds through operant conditioning as the environment conditions us.

The behaviorists' model is built on the pleasure—pain principle. We can be conditioned by our environment because we seek pleasure and avoid pain.

The behaviorists' view of human nature leads them to believe that one's behavior is the mirror of our environment and in its control, our behavior patterns are normative in nature so that, given sufficient numbers of organisms, normative behavior can be predicted with reasonable accuracy. Further, behaviorists believe that in time, they will know enough about one's behavior to be able to predict the behavior of specific individuals.

For the behaviorists, since a person is molded and controlled by the environment, it follows that one is not responsible for one's behavior. The responsibility falls on the shoulders of society, for we can only behave as we have been conditioned to behave.

The behaviorists see us locked in a deterministic structure within which we function as we are reinforced. Thus, we are incapable of any altruistic behavior, including love.

## PSYCHOANALYTIC: SIGMUND FREUD (1916), ALFRED ADLER (1958), ERIC ERIKSON (1994)

The basic model of the psychoanalysts is a psychodynamic model patterned after a hydraulic system: energy in the form of unconscious sexual—aggressive drives is channeled into creative or disruptive behavior.

The psychoanalysts see humans basically as passive individuals differing very little from other animals who are driven by internal, unconscious, sexual—aggressive forces and who react to external stimuli from the environment. There is a constant conflict between such internal and external forces, and our behavior can only be explained in terms of unconscious mental forces.

The psychoanalysts also maintain a response-dominated view of humans. But since such responses are caused by unconscious mental forces operating in conjunction with external stimuli and since those responses can be disguised in many ways, one can only infer what the cause of specific behaviors may be.

Based on Freud's behavioral model, psychoanalysts have put great faith in their ability to infer what mental processes are responsible for certain behaviors. These behaviors and the processes lying behind them have been explained by Freud in terms of three divisions of personality: the id, the ego, and the superego. The psychoanalysts' model is of an individual who has developed a homeostatic relationship between the id and the superego, a relationship which is governed by the ego.

The psychoanalysts see humans as irrational, as driven by unconscious forces beyond their complete control. Though we may behave rationally much of the time, we are always subject to irrational urges to gratify our basic drives.

The psychoanalysts' model is quite the reverse of the pleasure—pain principle, for it sees the individual as being controlled by internal forces, our unconscious sexual and aggressive drives. This view removes environment as the cause of behavior. Instead, environment becomes an adversary against which we must constantly fight.

The psychoanalysts' view that human nature is determined by internal forces leads to the conclusion that the prediction of one's behavior on a group basis is the result of the quantity of subjects participating in the study, rather than the predictability of human behavior. Since we may (and often do, socially) disguise the behavior resulting from our sexual or aggressive urges, it is impossible to predict an individual's behavior in any given instance.

For the psychoanalysts, since overt behavior is the result of unconscious drives, the individual is not responsible for his or her behavior. The responsibility lies with our unconscious urges, of which we are victims. The psychoanalysts' assumption is that because we are at the mercy of our psychosexual—aggressive drives, we can only attempt to satisfy these drives. Thus, we cannot perform loving altruistically, but only for self-gratification.

## HUMANISTIC: MASLOW (1968)

"The main thing in life is not to be afraid to be human."

—Pablo Casals

The basic model of the humanists is a cognitive-affective model which is uniquely human (anthropomorphic). We are assumed to develop intellectual and emotional structures, of which we can be aware and in control.

The humanists see humans as basically active in that we have a will of our own, are aware of our self-concepts, and have a potential for growth. We differ from other animals in a number of ways and are, thus, referred to as persons, rather than organisms. Our behavior can only be understood in relation to the whole person acting within a context.

The humanists have a generative-dominated view of humans in that they believe we can creatively adapt to any situation, and not just respond to it. Further, we actively seek growth experiences by anticipating events, checking our perceptions of the event with our anticipations, and modifying our thinking to agree with these tests of reality. Only we know why we behave the way we do, because only we know our intentions.

The humanists view the human being as developing through the cognitive growth of a self-directing system; that is, the cognitive structure of a person is built through a process using feedback. Since it is self-regulating, it is subject only to its own limitations and is responsible for the resulting mental structure.

The humanist model is of a person who may become aware of and move toward his or her fullest potential. This self-actualization is prompted by the humanistic conscience—the awareness of one's potential, as a human being, to mature as a person and to contribute to the healthy growth of society.

The humanist view of human beings is that we are rational because we are aware of the self and of our social embeddedness. This view implies that we must control our behavior with both of these factors in mind. Thus, we do not accentuate the one to the detriment of the other. The humanistic view is that humans control themselves and their environment through their own reasoning processes. We can be autonomous beings (self-governed and self-determined), neither driven by internal forces nor manipulated by external ones.

The humanistic approach is that although the normative behavior of masses of people may be predictable, an individual's behavior is not, because of one's freedom of choice. The humanists' meaning of predictable is at a deeper level than the behaviorists. Humanists believe that many people may behave overtly in the same way, but that each will have a different reason for behaving that way. Thus, our choice (behavior) is not predictable. Further, since we are free to make choices, we may choose not to make the same choice the next time.

The humanist model sees the person as responsible for his or her behavior. If we are autonomous, aware of self and society, and have freedom of choice, then we must be responsible for our actions.

The humanistic model presents the ideal person as being able to transcend "self" in order to enter into meaningful relationships through involvement with others and into commitment to a love greater than "self." In these three perspectives we are introduced to the gate way to introduce communication. Through instruction, exposure to different speeches, feedback, and individual learning experiences, students will be able to understand their communicative environment, secure and adapt to their unconscious mental forces and become more humanistic in fulfilling their basic needs.

## SUGGESTED ACTIVITIES

### Behaviorist Activities

Analyze the environment in which you live:

a) What elements affect your behaviors over which you have no (or very little) control?

b) What elements in your environment affect your behaviors because you choose to let them do so?

Does the environment control your behavior? List ten examples of your behavior in each environment (home and college) and indicate how these behaviors differ. What do these behaviors have to do with communication?

Join a group of other students and attempt to create an environment you feel would greatly enhance the chances for children to develop a positive concept of themselves. List the major items you would include in such an environment.

## Psychoanalytic Activities

In the area of sports, particularly individual sports such as boxing or gymnastics, many feel that sexual intercourse during the twenty-four hours preceding an athletic event is detrimental to the performance of the individual.

a)  How strongly do you feel about this subject?
b)  Do athletes take this as a fact or a superstition?
c)  It is considered equally valid for male and female athletes?

In what ways do you orient your life around sexual relationships, goals and intentions? List ten ways in which this orientation affects your communicative behavior. Are they the same for males and females?

## Humanistic Activities

As a group, rank the following characteristics in the order you feel they are important, marking the most important and the least important ones:

Caring
Constructive
Compassionate
Discriminating
Egocentric
Straightforward
Ambitious
Accomplished
Goal oriented
Energetic
Capable
Predictable
Loyal
Friendly
Courteous
Reverent

List the ways you feel the human being differs from lower forms of animal life. Where do freedom of choice and control of the environment fit?

One of the oldest questions asked by humans, going back at least to the time of Plato, has to do with the nature of reality. "What is real?" is a question which has been answered in many different ways throughout history. Some have claimed that our physical world is "real" and the task of perception is to discover what is "out there." Others have argued that the physical world is only a figment of our imagination, based on images which can be created at will by the perceiver. While the debate on the nature of the physical world will probably continue, there is emerging consensus that social reality is primarily based on perception. The three views of human nature describe how our social reality is constructed through our communication with others.

Researchers in communication are concerned with how our actions are guided by "constructs" which help us understand and anticipate events, thereby coping with the world around us. Constructs are formed through the process of anticipating events and experiencing the consequences.

If a construct proves useful, we will probably keep it and use it again in a similar event. If it does not help us understand our world we will probably discard it and try another one, or at least modify it so it works better the next time. I argue that we have a great deal of flexibility in choosing our constructs than we usually think we have. We might be able, to transform how we experience our social world if we simply construed them differently.

In essence, analysis of constructs mean we have much to say about events because we can choose the meanings we attach to them. We are not bound by the events themselves, but only by our perception of them. We make sense out of the world by listening, observing, tasting, touching, and smelling, then sharing our conclusions with others with both words and unspoken expressions. As noted, the message sent may not be the message received. Human communication encompasses many media: speeches, songs, radio and television broadcasts, e-mail, internet, letters, books, articles, poems and advertisements.

*Chapter Two*

# Definition and Values of Communication

## DEFINITION

Communication is one of those words that seem so basic that you may wonder why it needs to be formally defined. Yet scholars who devote their time to studying communication sometimes do not agree on the definition. In its broadest sense, communication is the process of acting on information. Someone does or says something, and others think or do something in response to the action or the words as they understand them. Communication involves making common.

## INTRODUCTION

According to Wood (2001), communication is a systematic process in which individuals interact with and through symbols to create and interpret meaning. Process means communicative interaction is ongoing and always in motion. It is hard to tell when communication starts and stops, since what happened long before we talk with someone may influence interaction and since what occurs in a particular encounter may have repercussions in the future. The fact that communication is a process means it is always in motion, moving ever forward and changing continuously. We cannot freeze communication at any one moment.

Systematic means that communication involves a group of interrelated parts which affect one another. In family communication, for instance, each member of the family is part of the system. To interpret communication, we have to consider the entire system in which it takes place.

Symbols are abstract, arbitrary, and ambiguous representations of other things. Symbols include all of language and many nonverbal behaviors, as well as art and music. Anything that abstractly signifies something else can be a symbol. We might symbolize love by giving someone a ring that says, "I love you," or by taking someone out for a special dinner. Human communication involves individuals who use symbols to interact with themselves and each other.

Meanings are the heart of communication. Meanings are not intrinsic in experience. Instead, we create them, typically in the process of communication. We talk with others to clarify our own thoughts, to decide how to interpret nonverbal behaviors, and to put labels on feelings and hopes so that they have reality. One can safely say that human communication is the process of making sense out of the world and sharing that sense with others through verbal and nonverbal messages.

In all of these ways, we actively construct meaning by working with symbols.

## VALUES OF COMMUNICATION

We spend more time communicating than doing anything else. We talk, listen, have dialogues with ourselves, watch television and listen to radio, participate in group discussions, browse the worldwide web, interview or are interviewed, send electronic mail messages, and so forth. From birth to death, we communicate to meet personal, professional, relationship, and social goals.

Personal Impact. George Mead (1934) said that "Humans are talked into humanity." He meant that we gain personal identity through communicating with others. We first see ourselves through the eyes of others, so their messages are extremely important in forming the foundations of self-concept.

Later in life, we interact with peers and teachers, who communicate how they see us; and we filter their impressions into our own self image. Interactions with friends and romantic partners provide additional insight into how others see us, thus, how we see ourselves. Mass communication—including radio, television, and films—also influences our understandings of ourselves and the world.

Wood (2006) adds that the profound connection between identity and communication is dramatically evident in children who are deprived of human contact. Case studies of children who were isolated from others reveal that these children seem to have few signs of themselves as humans and that their mental and psychological development is severely hindered by lack of language. Communication with others not only affects our sense of identity, but also directly influences our physical well being. People who lack close friends have greater levels of anxiety and depression than people who are close to others. Heart disease is also more common among people who lack strong interpersonal relationships. Steve Duck (1991), a scholar of interpersonal communication, reports that people in disturbed relationships tend to have low self-esteem, headaches, alcoholism, cancer, sleep disorders, and other physical problems. Clearly, healthy interaction with others is important to our physical and mental health.

Relationship Impact. Communication also critically affects our relationships. We build connections with others by revealing our private identities, remembering shared history, planning a future, and working out problems and tensions. Marriage counselors have long emphasized the importance of communication for healthy, enduring relationships. Troubles and problems are not the primary reason why marriages fail, since those are common to all relationships. A primary distinction between relationships that endure that those that collapse is effective communication. Couples who have worked at understanding each other and who talk through problems have the potential to adjust and refine their relationships so that the relationships remain healthy over time.

Good communication in intimate relationships involves being a skillful listener, expressing ideas clearly, and responding with empathy and understanding. Talk is the essence of relational maintenance. Progression in the relationships between instructors and students, in terms of the communication, motivates and affects increases or decreases in uncertainty. Positive reinforcement comes by letting students know that the course means business, that they are accountable for learning. Rules Theory also adds that the instructor sets norms. There should be clear expectations for the discussion process. Key points are listed in writing, important information is shared, information is summarized, and all contributions from students are treated with respect.

Professional Impact. Communication skills affect professional success. The importance of communication is obvious in professions such as teaching, business, law, broadcasting, sales, and counseling, in which talking and listening are central. Career counselors tell us that many attorneys, counselors, business people, and teachers major or minor in communication before pursuing specialized graduate training. What they learn about ways to present their ideas and respond to the communication of others allows them to be persuasive, effective professionals. In other fields, the importance of communication is less obvious, but nonetheless present. Even highly technical work, such as computer programming, accounting, and systems design, requires a variety of communication skills. Specialists have to be able to get along with others and to explain their ideas—particularly technical ones—to people who lack their specialized knowledge. It is virtually impossible to think of a career that does not involve communication.

## MODELS OF COMMUNICATION

Several models of communication have been developed that reflect understanding of communication processes.

The linear model describes communication as one way. The model portrays communication as flowing in only one direction. Linear views can be inaccurate because communication processes are bidirectional and hence might impede processes.

Interactive models are sometimes based on the realization that listeners respond to senders through the process of feedback. Feedback is a receiver's response to a message. It may be verbal or nonverbal; it may be intentional or unintentional. The bottom line in interaction is that both senders and receivers participate and identify meaning through the process of feedback. The interactive model designates one person as sender and another person as receiver. In reality, both send and receive messages verbally and nonverbally.

A perspective of the transactional model emphasizes that communication occurs within systems that affect what and how people communicate and what meanings they create. A transactional model emphasizes the use of systems, or context, including shared systems of communicators and personal systems of each communicator. The transactional model does not label one person as sender and the other as receiver. Instead, communicators participate equally and simultaneously.

## CHARACTERISTICS OF COMMUNICATION

1. Communication is a process. This statement implies that communication does not have a beginning, an end, a fixed sequence of events. It is not static, at rest; it is moving. The ingredients within a process interact; each affects all of the others. Communication is both dynamic (constantly changing) and interactive.
2. Communication is complex. Being a process, communication is not as direct and one way. Rather, it proceeds on verbal and nonverbal levels in both directions. Furthermore, communication is complex because it involves so many variables or ingredients.

3. Communication is symbolic. One important characteristic of communication is that it involves the use of symbols of some kind. Symbols are arbitrary, man-made signs that represent thought. A given symbol means something different to everyone. Therefore, communication is not the simple transfer of thought from one person to another. Rather, it is a process in which one individual encodes or translates his thoughts into a symbol and sends that message via some medium to a receiver. The receiver then translates the message into thought (decodes the symbol). Thought and meaning are not transferred—messages are.

   Not all symbols are words. For instance, "thumbs down", long hair, and sarcastic voice inflection are all symbols that communicate ideas or a set of ideas.

4. Communication is a receiver phenomenon.
   A. Communication always occurs in the receiver.
   B. If communication occurs within the receiver, the intention of the sender is largely unimportant.
   C. We ought to examine the types of responses that occur.
   D. Communication occurs when the receiver attaches meaning to others' behavior. "One cannot not communicate." All behavior, when perceived by another, has potential message value or communicative significance.

5. Communication is transitory. Communication is irreversible. It can only go onward; it cannot back up and try again.

   Communication is unrepeatable. Even if the message is repeated word for word, the audience has been changed by the first attempt. Therefore, different receivers might attach a different meaning to the same message.

   Because communication is much more than stimulus and response, cause and effect, action and reaction, it is best viewed as "transaction" a process in which the exchange of messages serves to define the relationship between individuals.

# Chapter Three

# Self-Concept

If you cannot become your best, you cannot be happy,
If you cannot risk, you cannot grow,
If you cannot grow, you cannot become your best,
If you cannot become your best, you cannot be happy,
If you cannot be happy, what else matters?
David Viscott, M.D.

(From Risking, 1988)

Most scholars will agree that we have a core of behaviors, attitudes, beliefs and values that constitute our self–the sum total of who we are.

A component in the belief-attitude value system that assumes great overall importance is the self-concept. Self-concept consists of one's beliefs about the self. It is the individual's answer to the question, "What am I?" Self-concept is particularly important to the system because, the ultimate purpose of one's total belief system, which includes one's values, is to maintain and enhance the sentiment of self regard. Thus, while beliefs, attitudes, and values constitute the components of the system, the self-concept is its guiding goal of purpose. The self is a "core" notion in terms of identity and discourse. The implication is that in interactions and transactions, the self-concept of the sender might determine the messages they send and that of the receiver may determine the assigned meaning. Identity plays a key role in communication, serving as a bridge between culture and communication

There are three components of the self: the material self, the social self, and the spiritual self.

*The material self* is a total of all of the tangible things you own: Your body, your possessions, and your home. When there is a discrepancy between our desired material self and our self-concept, we may respond to eliminate the discrepancy.

*The social self* is that part of you that interacts with others. Each relationship that you have with another person is unique because you bring to it a unique social self.

*The spiritual self* consists of internal thoughts and introspections about your values and moral standards. It is not dependent on what you own or with whom you talk. It is the essence of who you think you are, and of your feelings about yourself. It is a mixture of spiritual beliefs and your sense of who you are in relation to other forces in the universe. It is an attempt to understand inner essence, whether that essence is consciousness, spirit or soul. Your spiritual self is the part that answers the question, "Why am I here?"

Understanding the material, social and spiritual self might involve coping, adapting and the negotiation of identity. There might be effects of self constructs in the interpretation and production of meaning.

The self-concept is at the very heart of the communication process. Its influence strongly affects most behavior. What we see and hear how we think and feel and how we respond to others are all dependent on how we think and feel about ourselves.

## SELF-CONCEPT AND ATTITUDES

There is a relationship between the self concept and attitudes. Attitude refers to a predisposition to respond to stimuli in a particular way. Attitudes reflect what you like and what you don't like. Because many attitudes are formed quickly and often with little evidence, they are relatively susceptible to change through additional evidence and experience Attitudes and values function internally. They cannot be seen or touched (e.g., love).

Attitudes and values affect behavior, which is observable action.

Attitudes and values involve both feelings and ideas.

Attitudes and values vary in strength and specificity.

Attitudes and values organize concepts.

## DEVELOPMENT OF SELF-CONCEPT

Self awareness is a process that continues throughout life, as we perceive and come to understand our own existence in the social world. The way we view ourselves is termed self concept which includes our attitudes, beliefs, and values.

The self-concept develops through one's interactions with other people and the groups with which we associate.

1. Awareness of self
   Self awareness occurs as children learn to distinguish between sensations and the conditions that produce them. Children learn to recognize body parts, name feelings and behaviors as parts of a single self. Slowly, they begin to understand the meaning of "me."
2. Awareness of others
   Modeling: Observing the environment and imitating the behaviors
   Role Playing: Acting the observed behavior related to the role
3. Developing self identification
   Role taking: Internalizing of role-related behaviors and motivations
   Gender roles: Expectations for the behavior of men and women based on the person's sex
4. Others provide the looking glass
   Significant others: Persons whose attitudes toward us strongly influence our own thoughts and feelings about ourselves.
   Generalized others include composite view one may have of others' view of you.
5. Lifelong development: Self-concept is not static; it changes with life experiences.

## COMMUNICATION AND SELF-CONCEPT

1. Pygmalion effect: Greek myth—Others' expectations affect our behavior and communication.
2. Self-fulfilling prophecy: We all tend to behave as we expect ourselves to behave.

### Self-concept and cultural perception

The self-concept is developed through interactions with other people. The self-concept tends to resist change when one relates to other cultures. Cultural differences make the potential for misunderstanding even greater. The self-fulfilling prophecy is noted as having an influence on the relationship between self-concept and culture. Thus, an expectation of success will lead to greater effort in an intercultural situation, which, of course, will increase the chances of success. Culturally sensitive communication can increase relational and family closeness and deepen cultural self awareness.

## If . . .

If children live with criticism, they learn to condemn.

If children live with hostility, they learn to fight.

If children live with fears, they learn to be apprehensive.

If children live with pity, they learn to feel sorry for themselves.

If children live with jealousy, they learn to feel guilty.

If children live with encouragement, they learn to be confident.

If children live with tolerance, they learn to be patient.

If children live with praise, they learn to be appreciative.

If children live with acceptance, they learn to love.

If children live with approval, they learn to like themselves.

If children live with recognition, they learn to have a goal.

If children live with fairness, they learn what justice is.

If children live with honesty, they learn what truth is.

If children live with security, they learn to have faith in themselves and in those about them.

If children live with friendliness, they learn that the world is a good place in which to live.

*The Watchman-Examiner*
Harper & Row, Publishers, *the Treasure Chest; the Watchman-Examiner.*

## SUGGESTED ACTIVITIES

### Role Analysis

*Purpose*

To examine more closely the roles you play and how these roles affect aspects of communication.

*Procedure*

Answer the following questions individually; then we will discuss the responses as a class.

1. Try to list five of the roles which you commonly play, making each role separate and distinct from the others—i.e., student, mother, wife, etc.
2. How are each of the following altered by each of the above roles?
   a. Language
   b. Appearance
   c. Attitude
   d. Values
   e. Quantity and quality of communication

3. What major role expectations do you have for each of the following roles?
   a. Teacher
   b. Student
   c. Wife
   d. Husband
   e. Boy friend
   f. Girl friend
   g. Mother
   h. Father
   i. Son
   j. Daughter
   k. Clergyman
   l. Parishioner
   m. Doctor
   n. Patient
   o. Policeman
   p. Citizen
   q. Employer
   r. Employee
   s. Clerk
   t. Customer
4. Analyze the situations in Table 3.1 according to how different people might deal with them.
   a. What questions might each person ask?
   b. What factors would determine their reaction to each situation?

**Table 3.1.  Situations**

| How would a . . . | deal with . . . |
|---|---|
| Mother | buying a car |
| Father | selecting a college |
| Fashion model | seeing a ball game |
| Preacher | going on vacation |
| Boy friend | selling a boat |
| Girl friend | stealing an orange |
| Cab driver | punishing a small child |
| Salesperson | getting a speeding ticket |
| Police officer | going to the dentist |
| Rich student | paying a fine |
| Poor student | using leisure time |

## DISCUSSION

1. How do roles affect interpersonal communication?
2. Discuss role playing as a means of solving problems which occur in interpersonal communication situations.

This exercise is designed to highlight varied perceptions on how the many selves we have sometimes determine our communication.

### Your Many Selves

Objective: to become aware of some aspects of your many intercultural selves.

1. Self-concept can be compared to a many-faceted diamond. Each facet contributes to the brilliance of the stone, but each is separate. In this exercise, you will examine some of the facets of your self. Complete the statements as openly and honestly as you can. Note that how you complete the items is quite personal. You will need to share these responses with no one, unless you wish to do so.

### Thoughts and Attitudes

I believe that:

a. Religion is . . .
b. Religion should be . . .
c. Politics is . . .
d. Politics should be . . .
e. Women are . . .
f. Women should be . . .
g. Men are . . .
h. Men should be . . .
i. I am . . .
j. I should be . . .
k. I want to be . . .
l. My wife (husband) is . . .
m. My wife (husband) should be . . .
n. My girlfriend (boyfriend) is . . .
o. My girlfriend (boyfriend) should be . . .

## Feelings

a.  I am happy when I . . .
b.  I am sad when I . . .
c.  Next Saturday night I want to . . .
d.  Five years from now, I want to . . .
e.  I am happy when my wife (husband) . . .
f.  I am happy when my parents (children) . . .
g.  I am happy when my girlfriend (boyfriend) . . .
h.  I am sad when my wife (husband) . . .
i.  I am sad when my parents (children) . . .
j.  I am sad when my girlfriend (boyfriend) . . .

## Perceptions of Physical Aspects

a.  I am attractive (handsome) when . . .
b.  My . . . is attractive (handsome).
c.  My . . . . is ugly.
d.  My . . . is sexy.
e.  I am ashamed of my . . .
f.  I am proud of my . . .
g.  I am unattractive when . . .
h.  If I were a movie star, I could play the kind of roles that . . . does.
i.  I look terrible in . . .
j.  If I could change my looks, I would . . .
k.  I wish my voice were . . .
l.  The worst thing about my voice is . . .
m.  The best thing about my voice is . . .
n.  If I could change my voice, it would sound like . . .
o.  If I could change my walk, I would walk like . . .

## Values

a.  I am good at . . .
b.  I have trouble with . . .
c.  I love . . .
d.  I like . . .
e.  . . . should be destroyed.
f.  . . . are the most important things in life.
g.  I want . . .
h.  People are . . .

## DISCUSSION QUESTIONS

The following discussion questions involve processing in experiential learning. Students are to reflect on their experiences after doing the previous questionnaire.

a. How can awareness of the many facets of self-concept help you improve your ability to communicate?

b. What are the most important principles illustrated by, or learned from, this exercise?

Source: Anita Taylor (1988), *Communicating*

The Johari Window is a convenient way to categorize our knowledge or perceptions of ourselves. It can be useful by helping us focus on obtaining more knowledge (feedback) from others and helping us work on ways to share more information about ourselves with others. The Johari Window shows what people are willing to talk about and with whom.

By directing our information search and our information sharing efforts, the Johari Window can help us develop a healthier self-image and a more open and self-disclosing interpersonal communication style. The Johari Window is a "giftie," as one would say, a little gift, but it can prove of great value if used well.

### Self-Image Inventory

Our sense of personal adequacy cannot, of course, be measured on any absolute scale. We feel confident about some things, shaky about others. The Self-Image Inventory is designed to help describe how people think and feel about themselves. This self-test is an indication of your self-esteem, perception of yourself related to others, and satisfaction with your role in life.

There are no right or wrong answers, and you are encouraged to respond to each statement as honestly as you can. Circle the letter you feel best fits you. Complete the test, and score according to the number scale at the end.

**Table 3.2. The Johari Awareness Model**

| | |
|---|---|
| I. Open Self   *Things we both know about me* | II. Blind Self   *Things I don't recognize about myself but others do* |
| III. Concealed Self   *Things I don't want to or can't share about myself* | IV. Unknkown Self   *Things neither of us knows about me* |

This inventory is not intended to be used as a diagnostic test, but represents an inventory of self awareness and exploration.

1. In terms of attractiveness, I am:
   a. very attractive
   b. fairly attractive
   c. average
   d. passing
   e. unattractive
2. My personality is:
   a. very interesting
   b. fairly interesting
   c. average
   d. passing
   e. dull
3. I have:
   a. much confidence in myself
   b. enough confidence in myself
   c. average confidence in myself
   d. little confidence in myself
   e. no confidence in myself
4. I think that I get along with others:
   a. extremely well
   b. fairly well
   c. well enough
   d. not very well
   e. very poorly
5. When competing with others, I feel:
   a. I will usually win
   b. I have a good chance to win
   c. I will win sometimes
   d. I will usually not win
   e. I will probably never win
6. I dress:
   a. very well
   b. fairly well
   c. average
   d. don't care
   e. sloppy
7. When I walk into a room, I make a:
   a. good impression
   b. fair impression

    c. average impression

    d. no impression

    e. dull impression

8. I accept personal compliments with:

    a. no embarrassment

    b. little embarrassment

    c. occasional embarrassment

    d. frequent embarrassment

    e. constant embarrassment

9. With the opposite sex, I get along:

    a. very well

    b. fairly well

    c. average

    d. not very well

    e. very badly

10. In terms of maturity, I am:

    a. very mature

    b. fairly mature

    c. average

    d. below average

    e. immature

11. When among strangers, I feel:

    a. very comfortable

    b. fairly comfortable

    c. the same as usual

    d. uncomfortable

    e. extremely uncomfortable

12. I feel warm and happy toward myself:

    a. all of the time

    b. most of the time

    c. some of the time

    d. hardly ever

    e. none of the time

13. If I could make myself over, I would be:

    a. exactly as I am

    b. about the same

    c. slightly changed

    d. greatly changed

    e. another person

14. I experience enjoyment and zest for living:

    a. all of the time

    b. most of the time

    c. some of the time
    d. hardly ever
    e. none of the time

15. I admit my mistakes, shortcomings, and defeats:
    a. all of the time
    b. most of the time
    c. occasionally
    d. hardly ever
    e. none of the time

16. I usually feel inferior to others:
    a. none of the time
    b. hardly ever
    c. occasionally
    d. most of the time
    e. all of the time

17. I feel I am in control of my life:
    a. all of the time
    b. most of the time
    c. some of the time
    d. very little of the time
    e. none of the time

18. I have an intense need for recognition and approval:
    a. none of the time
    b. hardly ever
    c. occasionally
    d. most of the time
    e. all of the time

19. When I first meet people, they:
    a. like me very much
    b. like me well enough
    c. have an average impression
    d. have no impression
    e. dislike me

20. In terms of body-image, I:
    a. like myself as I am
    b. like my sex
    c. am not sure
    d. dislike myself
    e. prefer a different sex

Note: the SI Inventory is not intended to be used as a diagnostic test, but represents an inventory for self-awareness and exploration. The SI Inventory provides an instrument for examining different aspects of self-image and can provide a reference point for self-image insight and change.

Shaw and Renee (1997) examine the relationship between self concept and presentation in males and females. Participants in a study were asked to describe themselves on a checklist and then told a narrative that was content analyzed to determine self defining characteristics. On examining results, the authors argue that the self concepts of males and females are similar, but their narrative reveals more gender typed presentations. Examining persons' self concept might provide a fresh understanding of their most basic thoughts and values and presentation of familiar other is a reflection of self concept.

*Chapter Four*

# Perception

"You can see a lot by observing"

— Yogi Berra

Perception involves taking in stimuli through our senses, and it includes three components: attention and selection, organization, and interpretation. Perception is the process by which a person screens, selects, organizes, and interprets stimuli so that they have meaning. It is a process one uses to make sense out of one's environment so that a person can make the appropriate behavioral responses.

The nature of the relationship between students and what they learn in corresponding communication patterns is largely a matter of perception. The key question for any relationship is how the partners perceive and understand their interaction. The meaning generated from a communication situation is also constrained by our perception of the other people involved in the communication situation.

Several aspects of the person influence meaning. It is important to evaluate the communicator's purpose. Another major factor is trust among people in a variety of communication contexts. It is sufficient to say here that the reputation or experience we have had with a fellow communicator will go far to influence the meanings we generate in a given situation.

There are two primary approaches to organizing impressions of other people. The first assumes that traits interact with each other to form the total picture of a person. Traits are not independent of each other; rather, they combine and assume relative importance to form the overall impression. The second approach to organizing impressions is based on ideas about the behavior that characterizes particular types of people or about how people should behave in certain situations. Everyone has ideas about how certain types of people-such as extraverts, shy people, students, teachers, and parents-should behave.

In terms of theoretical implications, perception is related to the Uncertainty Theory. Berger (1991) and his colleagues argue that one of the primary functions of communication is the reduction of uncertainty. They believe that for most people, the need to attain knowledge and understanding of others is a powerful force. Berger's model is an interesting description of information-gathering processes and may help answer the question of how communication is used to predict behavior and to achieve social control.

## DEFINING PERCEPTION AND RELATING IT TO COMMUNICATION

Perception, according to Weaver (1968), is "the detection, registration, processing, and elaboration of environmental characteristics" "The beauty of this definition," says Weaver (1968), "is that it includes all within our environment that we detect, register, process, and elaborate" Weaver's definition of perception can be further simplified as, "the process of gathering information and giving it meaning".

Communication and perception are so closely related that we can't really mention one without the other. To understand interpersonal communication, we need some understanding of perception, for it is through perception that we become aware of our surroundings, give meaning to our world, and come to know ourselves and others" . . .

Perception is a complex activity; but by understanding the process, we can improve our chances for more effective interpersonal communication. We can expand the perimeters of our own personal world. Knobloch and Theiss (2006) examine the role of intimacy in the production and perception of relationship talk within courtship. The authors define relationship talk as content messages that reference the nature of the relationship between people. They conceptualize relationship talk in ways that attend to its nuances, and evaluating how intimacy predicts the production and perception of relationship. The authors conducted an observational study of conversations between 120 dating couples considering length of romantic interest, compared to intimacy. In general the results were that relationship talk was positively associated with people's perceptions of the relational impact of conversation.

1. Perception is not a passive process.
2. Perceptions can and do change.

3. We have much room for new material.
4. We do not accept stimuli just as they are presented.
5. Whatever meaning we are left with is based on how we process and assign attributes to the information, rather than on what actually happened.

## FACTORS THAT AFFECT THE RECEPTION OF STIMULI

Our perceptual categories develop as we grow in relation to our interests, experiences, and knowledge. Our culture, parents, religion, education, and peers are probably the strongest influences on how we perceive the world.

"Each individual's system depends on numerous elements that either broaden or limit the size of the categories. Our physiological makeup affects how much information we are able to gather . . . The kind of information we perceive is strongly affected by our expectations, attitudes, values, interests, emotions, needs, language, experience, and knowledge."

### Meanings Are In Us

Our interpretation of something is just that—an interpretation. Objects, events, and words do not have inherent meanings. Their meanings are in us, in the way we evaluate them. When we talk with someone else, we make up what that person says just as when we see an object, we make up what that object looks like. Raines and Craig (2007) develop theoretical models of receiver responses to anonymous communication. They tell us that the context of the communication involves perceptions of the source, message, and medium.

### Perceiving and Understanding

1. Perception is an active process of selecting, organizing and interpreting phenomena.
   a. Selection is the process of choosing which aspects of reality to notice.
      i. We notice things that stand out because they are intense, large, or unusual.
      ii. We can talk to ourselves to influence what we selectively attend.
      iii. Our needs, interests and motives also influence what we selectively perceive.
   b. Organization occurs when we use cognitive schemata to arrange perceptions in meaningful ways.
      i. Prototypes define the clearest, most representative examples of categories.

      ii. Personal constructs are bi-polar dimensions of judgment we use to assess phenomena.

      iii. Stereotypes are predictive generalizations about phenomena.

      iv. Scripts are sequences of action that reflect our expectations of how we and others will behave in specific situations.

  c. Interpretation is the subjective process of creating explanations for what we observe and experience.

      i. Attributions are explanations of why people act as they do.

        1. Dimensions of attributions are internal or external locus, stability, and controllability.

        2. Self-serving bias occurs when attributions serve the self-interests of the person constructing the attribution.

      ii. Attributions are subjective; they are not factual explanations of others' behavior.

2. Perception is influenced by many factors.

  a. Physiological factors shape perceptions.

  b. Expectations influence perceptions.

  c. Cognitive abilities affect how and what we perceive.

      i. Cognitive complexity refers to the number of constructs used, how abstract they are, and how elaborately they interact in our efforts to interpret phenomena.

      ii. Person-centeredness is the ability to perceive and act toward another as a unique individual.

  d. Social roles shape our perceptions.

  e. Cultural factors influence perceptions.

3. Four guidelines can improve skills in perceiving.

  a. Avoid mind reading, which is assuming you understand what another person thinks.

  b. Check perceptions with others.

  c. Distinguish facts from inferences.

  d. Monitor the self-serving bias.

As communicators we depend on our perceptions of other human beings in almost every aspect of our daily lives. The way we perceive others determines the kind of communication that takes place between us; in some cases, it even determines whether communication takes place at all.

We cannot take in everything. That is, we perceive only part of the available stimuli.

The inherent structures of our sense organs—our perceptual filters—limit our capacity to perceive. These limitations exist whether we are experiencing an object or a person. Although we all have these limitations, they vary considerably from one individual to another.

Our past experiences influence what we select and the way we perceive it.

Expectations, or psychological sets, have a profound effect on our perceptions of objects. For example, a defensive person is more apt to perceive strangers as hostile as a self-confident person is.

Perception does not necessarily lead to an accurate portrait of the environment, but rather to a unique portrait, influenced by the needs, desires, values, and disposition of the perceiver.

Two important aspects of the perceptual process should be noted: Perceptual selectivity, and perceptual organization. Perceptual selectivity is the process by which individuals single out, or select, certain objects in the environment for attention. Perceptual selectivity can be diagrammed as follows:

$$\text{Exposed} \rightarrow \text{Direct Attention} \rightarrow \text{Perceive} \rightarrow \text{Retention}$$

Perceptual organization occurs when individuals have attached meaning to an object. Then they are in a position to determine an appropriate response or reaction to it. For example, if we clearly recognize that the rock falling from the cliff above us may indeed cause us harm, we can quickly move away to safety.

## SOCIAL PERCEPTIONS IN ORGANIZATION

Social perceptions consist of those processes by which we perceive other people. The study of social perception places particular emphasis on how we interpret other people, how we categorize them, and how we form impressions of them. Accurate perception of others has great significance. There are four basic influences on the way we perceive other people.

### Characteristic of the Person Perceived

The first influence on how people are perceived in social situations is their own personal characteristics. It is clear that a variety of physical attributes influence how we are seen by others (by age, sex, race, height, and weight, for instance). In addition, what we say to others and how we say it can influence the impressions others form of us (verbal, nonverbal communication).

### Characteristic of the Situation

A second influence on how we perceive others is the situation in which the perceptual process occurs, as when people are given an opportunity to interact in a friendly and sociable work situation, they tend to see one another as similar to themselves.

## Characteristics of the Perceiver

Characteristics unique to our own personalities can affect how we see others. Our self-concept represents a major influence on how we perceive others. Our own personal characteristics influence the characteristics we are likely to see in others. For instance, people with authoritarian tendencies tend to view others in terms of power, while secure people tend to see others as warm, rather than cold.

## Barriers in Social Perception

Stereotyping, the Halo Effect, and selective perception are all barriers to communication. A stereotype assigns attributes to people solely on the basis of one or a few categories such as age, race, nationality, or occupation. Stereotypes often come into play when we meet new people, since we know very little about them at first. Stereotypes are not necessarily dysfunctional; and in some situations, they can be helpful. In unfamiliar social situations, we need general guidelines to assist us in interpreting our environment. While stereotypes have certain positive effects for the perceiver, they more often have detrimental effects for the person being perceived.

The Halo Effect is a tendency to allow knowledge of a trait to influence impressions of an individual's other traits. Halo effects, which can be either positive or negative, act as screens which inhibit perceivers from actually seeing the trait they may be judging.

Selective perception is the process by which we systematically screen information we don't wish to hear. Groups, for instance, tend to evaluate their own solutions as better than the solutions proposed by others.

## Improving Perception and Communication

Kockelman (2006) theorizes five interrelated processes that might account for key features of human modes: memories, perception, beliefs, intentions and plans. Because of variations in modes and cultures, perception checking skills help ensure that we are interpreting verbal and nonverbal behavior. Culture sensitive perception checking statements involve both direct and indirect contexts. Perception checking is part of mindful observation listening which are used cautiously in accordance with the particular topic, relationship, timing and situational context.

Failures in communication frequently occur because people have inaccurate perceptions of each other or because they are unaware that their perceptions are inaccurate. Perception and communication can be improved in several ways. One can facilitate interpersonal communication simply by improving the accuracy of perceptions. The three elements of perception (the perceiver, the object of perception, and the context within which the perception occurs) are so interwoven that one cannot be analyzed apart from the others. Improved perception and improved communication can occur only after the realization that perceptions are personal, subjective, and therefore, subject to error.

### Guidelines for Effective Perception

1. Look for various cues.
2. Note contradictory cues.
3. Delay forming conclusions.
4. Avoid mind reading.
5. Know one's own biases.
6. Check perceptions.

### SUGGESTED ACTIVITIES

### Perception: Agree/Disagree

*Purpose:*

To test your understanding of basic perception principles

*Procedure:*

1. Read each statement carefully.
2. If you believe it to be true, check the Agree column under individual. If you believe it, or any part of it, to be false, check the Disagree
3. For each of the statements in Table 4.1, check agree or disagree.

*Discussion:*

Your instructor will lead a discussion, comparing individual and group responses.

Empathy plays a role in perception. It is the process which makes it possible for participants in communication events to move toward functional level of understanding. The concept of empathy has been most fully developed in the field of psychology and counseling. It has been defined as personality characteristic, as accuracy in predicting internal states, emotional identification, and cognitive role-taking as communicating a sense of understanding to another.

**Table 4.1. Perception; Agree/Disagree**

| Individual | | | Group | |
|---|---|---|---|---|
| Agree | Disagree | | Agree | Disagree |
| | | 1. The perception of a physical object or event depends more upon the object or event than upon the mind of the observer. | | |
| | | 2. Perception is primarily an interpersonal phenomenon. | | |
| | | 3. The fact that hallucinations and dreams may seem as real as waking perception indicates that perception depends very little upon ex-External reality. | | |
| | | 4. The reaction we have to what we see generally depends upon learning and culture. | | |
| | | 5. We tend to see what we wish to see or are expecting to see, regardless of what reality is. | | |
| | | 6. We can eliminate all distortion in our perception by careful, scientific observation. | | |
| | | 7. Scientific instruments, though they extend the limits of our perceptions, do not make perception any more real. | | |
| | | 8. What we perceive is no more than a representation of what is. | | |
| | | 9. Perception is a physical response to a physical reality. It is only when we begin talking about our perceptions that we begin to distort them. | | |
| | | 10. If we are careful we can see the world as it really is. | | |
| | | 11. We react to our environment on the basis of what we perceive that environment to be like, and not on what the environment is really like. | | |

*Chapter Five*

# Language

Language is an institution of a community. Our sense of meaning can be denotative or connotative. Denotative meanings refer to the literal level of meaning and have primary associations for most members of a community. With connotative meanings, only a few members share meanings. It might be more appropriate to be denotative when we use language.

It is important to have effective verbal communication with others. The words we choose have great power to communicate. Who we are can influence the relationships we establish. Words are symbols with meanings that refer to objects, events, people and ideas. We interpret meanings through the culture and the context to which they belong. When we use language in communication in interactions and transactions, we affirm each other's uniqueness.

Every language is a group of codes that classifies experience. Coding, in the form of verbal language and nonverbal signs, is the raw material of communication. Our languages and other codes are rich in variation and meaning some have direct or indirect implications, and we adjust and adapt our verbal and nonverbal signals as we move from one setting to another.

Humans are continuously immersed in language. They can never escape from a realm that is inevitably symbolically mediated because our use of language affects our perceptions. In other words, it is impossible to think about ourselves, others, or situations without language. Further, the language that we use reflects and reproduces the values, social relations, and subject positions endorsed by our culture.

Although theorists insist that we exist as subjects only in and through language, they do not assume that any term or terms can completely describe a person. Instead, they believe that we can neither escape linguistic definition nor be totally described by it.

Using words is not simple. Trying to put our finger on the problems of using words is hard because so much depends on the users of the words and the contexts in which the words are used. And we have to use words even to describe the problems of using words. There is no way around it. Even if we understood all about users and contexts, we wouldn't have all the answers, because things will change. Words, as we have seen, are flexible in meaning. Our effectiveness in using them depends upon understanding how they can vary, depending on different communication contexts.

The purpose of Symbolic Interaction is to try to make clear that as humans, we belong to a peculiarly rule-making and rule-following, symbol-making, symbol-using, symbol-misusing species. Verbal communication has a tremendous impact on interpersonal relationships.

Language is symbolic, and we use symbols when we engage in verbal communication.

1. Symbols have three features.
   a. Symbols are arbitrary.
      i. They are not intrinsically connected to the phenomena they represent.
      ii. Meanings change over time.
      iii. New words are coined to represent new phenomena or revised perspectives on familiar phenomena.
   b. Symbols are ambiguous.
      i. Their meanings are not clear-cut.
      ii. Their meanings are not fixed for all time.
      iii. Connotative meanings vary among people.
   c. Symbols are abstract.
      i. They are not concrete, or tangible.
      ii. They vary in degree of abstractness.
      iii. The potential for confusion increases with increased abstractness.
2. There are 3 key principles of verbal communication.
   a. Interpretation creates meaning.
      i. Interpretation is an active, creative process.
      ii. Effective communicators are alert to possibilities of different interpretations among individuals.
   b. Communication is rule-guided.
      i. Regulative rules order interaction by specifying where, when, how, and with whom to talk about various topics.
      ii. Constitutive rules define what various types of communication mean, or count as.

   c. How we punctuate communication affects the meanings we attribute to it.

      i. Punctuation defines where communication episodes start and stop.

      ii. Punctuation is subjective, so there is no absolutely correct way to punctuate any interaction.

3. Six symbolic abilities affect our lives profoundly.

   a. Symbols define phenomena.

      i. The way we name, or define, phenomena shapes what they mean to us.

      ii. Totalizing occurs when we respond to a person as if one label totally represents what she or he is.

   b. Symbols evaluate phenomena.

      i. Symbols are not neutral.

      ii. Loaded language consists of words that strongly slant perceptions.

   c. Symbols organize experiences.

      i. We rely on cognitive schemata, which are symbols, to classify and evaluate phenomena.

      ii. Stereotypes involve thinking in broad generalizations about a whole class of people or phenomena.

   d. Symbols allow us to think hypothetically.

      i. We can think in all three dimensions of time, even though we exist in the present.

      ii. We can think of alternatives to what exists.

   e. Symbols allow us to reflect on ourselves.

      i. We are able to think about ourselves.

      ii. We are able to monitor our behavior.

      iii. The ME aspect of self is the socially aware self that reflects on the I, which is the naïve, creative, impulsive aspect of self.

   f. Symbols define relationships and interaction.

      i. Words are used to regulate interaction, for example, saying "excuse me," to enter a conversation.

      ii. Words can be used to represent power, liking, and responsiveness between communicators.

Source: Lisa Sparks, George Mason University

## LANGUAGE AND MEANING

Hudson (1980) in the Study of Language in Relationship to Society proposes that, language is one of the components creating, defining, and sustaining society. For example, Hudson has argued that language is an instrument of socialization. The language-society relationship implies that some sort of speech community exists in which people experience part of their sense of belonging to a society because they share a common language.

Bruce Gronbeck (1978) maintains that the sociolinguistic process presumes human beings are "symbol-using (symbol-making, symbol-misusing) animals, that symbols—and the society which invents, promulgates, and sanctions them—are determinative of any individual's perception or apprehension of the world, attitudes, values, and behaviors, and that humans are born into, nurtured by, and in large measure, controlled through a series of symbolic environments." Thus we see the energizing force of language upon societal structures.

Alfred Korzybski (1995) was concerned with general semantics, the relationships among what we say, what we think, and what we perceive in our environment. Holding that the special structure of language we acquire is because of environment and copying, Korzybski maintained that human thought processes or semantic reactions could be trained to avoid delusional values and reflect the objective level or reality as it was.

Richard Weaver (1967) claims in general semantics that language should conform as closely as possible to an external reality by being objective. He took the idealist stance that true rhetoric involves choices among values and courses of action; it aims at showing people better versions of themselves and better versions of an ultimate God. Weaver (1968) presented much of his philosophy in Ideas Have Consequences and in the Ethics of Rhetoric, in which he had his often-cited essay, Language is Sermonic because it allows choice making.

Weaver (1968) encouraged scholars to use ordinary language methods. Language has the nature of an open-ended institution.

Weaver (1968) recommended approaching language as constitutive, rather than just referential (words and meaning). Individual experiences constituted a component in the dynamic relationship between language and society.

## Language Paradigm

A language paradigm is an attempt to explain how we can find meaning in the context, in episodes and in symbolic acts.

Context specifies the criteria for interpreting both the meaningfulness and propriety of any communicative event. Two areas:

1. Form of Life imposes upon communication an aesthetic pattern which triggers expectations. Creation of an appetite in the mind of audience, expectations, cause-and-effect problem solving, etc., Form of Life exerts indirect social regulation upon communicative events. Rituals, ceremonies,

relationships among teachers and students, wives and husbands, executives and subordinates typified and constrained by the institutional structure found in Form of Life.

2. If communication becomes generally meaningful through knowledge, aesthetic, and institutional dimensions of Form of Life, communication becomes appropriate through a second level of context; namely, encounters. Encounters are points of contact among conscious humans. External signs of encounter are classrooms, bus depots, theaters, football stadiums, churches, restaurants or any concrete location.

The sufficient condition for an encounter is the acknowledgement of one another's presence. Encounters apply relevant Form of Life knowledge to each given situation. It will be the encounter which determines whether to abandon their common jargon in order to exchange, say, political views or local sports news.

Encounters provide practical significance to patterns through the communicative choices available. Encounters create particular expectations of form and also practical communicative means to fulfill those expectations.

## Episodes: Rule Conforming Sequences of Symbolic Acts

Three general features distinguish the construct of an episode.

1. Episodes are rule conforming to the extent that actors assume responsibility for free choice within any episode. Episodes activate the rules of each encounter.
2. Episodes relate to goal orientation.
3. Explanatory significance of their developmental structure. The centrality of episodes represents a conscious departure from those conceptions of communication which have elevated rapid eye movements, heading nodding to the status of central communication constructs and in so doing, have left the meaning of those constructs in question.

Episodic form defines the structure of communication. This structure is composed not of stylistic variations, but rather of a recurrent analytic base. Episodes typically begin with

1. An initiation imperative is usually the beginning or point of contact, and it involves acknowledgement of one another presence and willingness to enact an episode and usually involve verbal or nonverbal greetings and breaking the ice.

2. Definition occurs when both parties agree on the goal of the interaction. It involves consensual agreement upon what general type of episode will be enacted. Three types of episode may be enacted:
   a. Structurally dominant-quality of action defines the character of episode (e.g., formal introductions, turn taking procedures, interpersonal rituals).
   b. Informational dominant disclosure of knowledge to accomplish purposes (e.g., lecture, essay writing, etc.).
   c. Relationally dominant formation, confirmation, or undermining of personal relationships characterizes the episode (e.g., intimacy and disclosure acts, demonstrations of power distance, and the servicing of exclusively personal needs).
3. Rule confirmation signifies sometimes stated and implied rules and norms—e.g acquaintances who sit down for a poker game.
   a. Encounter activated rules sometimes deal with immediacy of situation.
   b. Experiment with alternative rules
   c. Overtly confirm
4. Strategic development involves working towards mutual and acceptable benefits in fulfilling needs and goals and depends on chosen acts and alternatives with parties having knowledge of both actual and potential choices in mutual fulfillment of emergent goals.
5. Termination is not necessarily the end, but is the point in determining if the relationship between communicants can be enhanced, repaired or ended and occurs whenever the goal dominating the previous imperative is accomplished, abandoned, or redefined. The definitive act of termination is to leave one another's presence expressing satisfaction with the accomplishment of goals, proposing the enactment of another episode.

## SYMBOLIC ACTS

Symbolic acts are verbal and (or) nonverbal utterances which express intentionality. Three properties of symbolic acts clarify their recognizable features.

a. Propositional force has a certain sense and reference which is approximately equivalent to formal semantic meaning.
b. Expressive force in the act of performing them. Expressive force is a situational function, such as promising, threatening, commanding, asserting, questioning, which each act performs.
c. Consequential force-effect.

Speech Act philosophy attempts to explain symbolic acts independently of the episodes in which they occur. A communicative understanding of symbolic acts demands an explanation of how such acts function in an episodic context.

The structure of the language action paradigm implies that communicative meaning is not inherent in individual symbolic acts. Rather, the overall form of an episode determines the overall meaning of a symbolic act.


## SUGGESTED ACTIVITIES

Distinguishing between facts and inferences is important in using verbal communication. Facts are observable; they can be verified and may have certainty. Inferences are opinions or guess which may not necessarily be true.

Circle the most appropriate letter: F for Fact; I for Inference:

1. He must be a good worker—they've kept him for 15 years.(F/I)
2. You seem sad.(F/I)
3. Yesterday, it rained 4.6 inches.(F/I)
4. The sun will rise tomorrow.(F/I)
5. He is a warm person.(F/I)
6. School closes when it snows.(F/I)
7. Hank is healthy.(F/I)
8. All women are illogical.(F/I)
9. This exercise is difficult.(F/I)
10. You are reading.(F/I)


### Fact vs. inference

*Objective*

To illustrate the difference between statements of fact (descriptions of observations) and statements of inference or opinion.

*Procedure*

Hold up an ordinary object (a fountain pen, a piece of clothing, textbook, piece of fruit, etc . . .) Ask participants to make statements of fact about the object. Record statements on the board. After getting ten or so items, point out that any that go beyond that which can be observed are inferences. Then ask what differences knowing and applying these might make during discussions.

# DISCUSSION QUESTIONS

1. What are the major differences between statements of fact, opinion, and (or) inference? Statements of fact are: limited to description, made only after observation, are limited in number that can be made; and if primary, can be made only by a direct observer. Statements of inference go beyond what is directly observed; can be made at any time without observation; can be made by anyone, observer or not; are unlimited in number about anything; and entail some degree of probability of inferential risk or uncertainty.)

2. Why is it especially important, both in gathering data and evaluating it during discussion, to distinguish between statements of inference or fact? (Recognise the danger for misunderstanding and ineffective communication when statements of inference are acted upon as if they were facts.)

3. Should both statements of fact and inference be treated with the same degree of certaintly? Why? Why not?

## Materials Required

Any handy item such as a pen, book, etc.

## Approximate Time Required

Fifteen to thirty minutes

## Source

Jacqueline V. Markus, Department of Communication, Arizona State University, Tempe, Arizona. Adapted from the Instructor's Manual, Effective Group Discussions, Fourth Edition, John Brilhart.

If one uses inferences, it is effective in communication to use qualifying statements such as:

As far as I know-
As I see it-
To my way of thinking-
It may be-
It seems to me-
I think

**Facts**

1. Exist or happen in the physical world.
2. Can be verified by one or more senses.

**Statements of Observation**

1. Describe facts, but are not themselves facts.
2. Are limited to what can actually be observed.
3. Can sometimes be verified by other observers.
4. Cannot be made about the future.

**Statements of Inference**

1. Go beyond describing.
2. Are not limited to observation, usually involve interpretation of something observed.
3. Cannot be verified by one or more senses; are tested by whether they meet logical standards or criteria.

## LANGUAGE AFFECTS PERCEPTION

Describe the following behavior and ask the class to brainstorm all the possible labels for each behavior. Put the brainstormed list on the board. The list should include terms that convey positive perceptions and negative perceptions of each behavior. Process the exercise by pointing out that our labels show our attitudes, convey our perceptions, and shape our subsequent perceptions of that same behavior.

a. Imagine an individual who earns $100 a week, saves $90 a week, and spends $10 a week. What words best describe that behavior? (frugal, thrifty, and so on)
b. Imagine a person who is 6 feet tall and weighs 120 pounds. What words would best describe this person? (thin, skinny, and so on)
   Time Limit: 20 minutes.

*Changing Words*

a. Form groups of five. Have each group discuss and complete the following questions:
b. What are five "new" words that have become popular in the last five years?

c. What are five old (obsolete) words that are no longer popular? (Think of unusual expressions used by older friends and relatives.)
d. What are five words that derive from an American subculture group?
e. What are five words with extremely negative emotional connotations in our society right now?
f. What are five common slang terms?

Have a spokesperson from each group share the lists with the entire class. Discuss according to the following questions.

a. Why do words change?
b. How do these words affect interpersonal communication?

Time Limit: 20 minutes for small group discussions/20 minutes for class discussion

*Portraits*

Choose one of the items listed below and describe it, using the seven kinds of imagery to create an evolving portrait of your listeners.

a. One of the scenes in your favorite movie
b. A tropical plant
c. A breakfast food
d. A complicated machine
e. The oldest building on campus

## Consider Your Relational Vocabulary

Step 1: Individually write out your definition or understanding of the following concepts as you think they apply to interpersonal relationships.

1. What is *stimulating* in a relationship?
2. What does *acceptance* mean in a relationship?
3. Define a *long-term relationship*
4. What is interpersonal *trust*?
5. What do you mean by *independence* in a relationship?
6. What is *security* in a relationship?
7. How would you describe *a fair relationship*?
8. Explain what you mean by *conflict*.
9. What do you think is *sexy*.
10. What do you define as *cheating*.

Step 2: Now in pairs or in groups go over the lists. Does everyone agree on the meanings? What is "right"?

## UNDERSTANDING DIVERSE LANGUAGE FUNCTIONS

The diverse functions of language are the world view function, the cognitive formation function, the social reality functions, the group identity function and the social change function.

To understand the world view function, we have to understand the language of a cultural group. To understand language in context, we have to understand the fundamental. Intercultural experts have proposed two world views that contrast the Western and Asian cultures: the linear world view and relational worldview.

A linear world view emphasizes rational thinking and is based on an objective reality. A relational worldview emphasizes holistic or connected thinking that is based on contextual reality. The language systems of the linear world view tend to emphasize either facts and figures or models and theories by using inductive and deductive reasoning.

The relational world view reflects a holistic reasoning pattern with connected thinking context based reasoning.

The cognitive formation language function serves as a mediating link between our cultural world views, on one hand and thinking patterns.

The Social function of language is that it serves as a gatekeeper in naming and selecting what is considered news or real in our social environment. We use particular language categories to name and label our everyday moments in our environment.

The group identity language function is that it represents a rallying point for evoking group sentiment and shared identity. Language serves the larger cultural ethnic identity function because it is an emblem of group solidarity.

The social change language function implies as innovative social beings, we are the creators of the social tool of human language.

Many who study language believe that it creates human realities with the relation to consciousness. Because language is a living process that reflects the lives of its users, it changes as the people who use it change.

There are cultural differences in verbal communication. Cultures vary in how much meaning is embedded in the language itself and how much meaning is interpreted from the context in which the communication occurs. Sometimes a way to check if the intended message is the perceived message is through the process of feedback. The most effective feedback should indicate to the sender that we are listening to the content of the message, interpreting it accurately, and understanding it. To give feedback, it is good to be constructive, sometimes talking about yourself, restricting your feedback to things you know for certain, providing positive feedback, as well as negative, understanding the content, not using labels being careful not to exaggerate and not being too judgmental. To receive feedback, breathe, listen, don't interrupt, and don't discourage the feedback giver. Ask questions for clarity or for specific examples. Acknowledge the feedback, paraphrase the message in your own words, acknowledge the valid points, and agree with what is true and take time to sort out what you have heard.

*Chapter Six*

# Non Verbal Communication

## NON VERBAL MESSAGE SYSTEMS

### Activity: Identifying Feelings

*Guidelines and descriptions for emotional expression*

Albert Mehrabian's (1972) work in non verbal communication claims that 93 percent of the emotional impact of a message comes from a non verbal source.

Successful communicators effectively use and interpret non verbal messages. Non verbal communication is central to our ability to function competently in relationships, because we convey our feelings and attitudes and detect the emotional states of others primarily through non verbal channels. Knapp and Hall (2002) describe the three primary types of non verbal communication that provide a continuous flow of messages. They stress the importance of physical context as well as the physical characteristics of communicators and their behaviors. Non verbal messages function with verbal messages in that they can substitute for, complement, contradict, repeat, regulate, and accent our words.

The more we think about non verbal communication and semiotics, the more we see how true it is that we cannot *not* communicate. Words come one at a time, but non verbal cues come continuously.

There are three well-tested assumptions that underlie any theory or set of theories about non verbal communication. One is that individuals develop expectations about the non verbal behavior of others. These expectations arise from social norms and from one's prior knowledge of a communicator's idiosyncrasies. (In the case of interactions with strangers, only the social norms dictate expectancies.) A second assumption is that communication behaviors have evaluations attached to them. Whether a specific behavior or collection of behaviors is placed within the positive or negative end of the evaluative continuum depends on the social community's values or standards and on individual preferences. For example, fluent speaking is positively valued in the culture of the United States; whereas, frequent touching from strangers is not. The evaluation of a behavior may be a function of what meanings are attached to it (e.g., frequent touching expresses high intimacy, which is inappropriate when coming from a stranger). This ties in to the third assumption—that non verbal behaviors have meanings. Some behaviors may have unitary and unambiguous meaning, and others may have multiple and possibly conflicting meanings; but it is assumed that the array of possible meanings is recognized within a social community. (A caress, for instance, may convey sympathy, comfort, dominance, affection, attraction, or lust.)

Signs, as semiotics suggest, are rarely treated as singular, independent units. Rather, organized or patterned systems of signs are required for communication as we know it. Even an isolated sign, such as a powerful word or non verbal gesture, can be understood by virtue of its differences from other signs. In fact, signs acquire meaning from the ways in which they are different from other signs within the system.

Non verbal communication is a topic of interest to communication scholars. Researchers have been intrigued with the ways in which non verbal systems are similar to and different from language. Knowledge of non verbal messages can affect how one communicates successfully in the real world. Although non verbal behaviors may be accompanied by verbal utterances, they both usually occur within a total communication context. Burgoon and Saine (1978) present six ways that the two codes work in conjunction: redundancy, substitution, complementation, emphasis, contradiction, and regulation.

Non verbal communication, which helps transmit feelings and emotions, regulates interaction with others, and works together with verbal communication to create messages. Non verbal communication has many aspects: physical appearance, facial gestures, eye behavior, touch, vocal characteristics, body movement, and the physical and psychological contexts within which each of these takes place. All of these aspects contribute to non verbal communication.

Accommodation Theory is useful in social interaction. One should therefore complement the verbal and non verbal according to how one believes others in the situation would best receive it.

Even though we may be unaware of much of it, non verbal communication is going on all the time. We experience non verbal messages in one of three languages: Sign language, action language, object language.

Sign language: when we deliberately use gestures to replace words or punctuation marks, e.g., peace sign or the hitch hikers' signal.

Action language: all the movements that we do not use exclusively as signals-walking, running, eating, etc.

Object language: the intentional or unintentional display of material things: art objects, machines, clothing, jewelry, etc.

Cultural Cues

Proxemics-space

Time

Visual Cues

Facial expression, eye contact, body movements, hand gestures, physical appearance

Vocal Cues

Volume, rate of fluency, pitch, quality

Non verbal Communication is communication without the use of words. It is governed by rules. It is important and rich in meaning. It continuously conveys emotions, and it emphasizes the question, "Do our actions match our words?"

1. The Rules of the Game
   a. There are certain kinds of behavior that we have been socialized to accept.
   b. Americans meet each other with "civil inattention," according to Erving Goffman (1959). We take enough visual notice of others to let them know that we know they are there, but not enough notice to seem curious or to intrude.
   c. Non verbal messages pack much meaning into otherwise small looks and gestures.
   d. All non verbal communication is influenced by a variety of factors: our personality, the situations we are in, the attitudes we hold toward people, the pecking order we maintain with others, and our cultural upbringing.
   e. Non verbal components almost always operate in conjunction with one another.
   f. We draw conclusions from numerous non verbal signals simultaneously and we do it very quickly. Whether the conclusions are accurate or inaccurate, we seldom have time to check.
2. The Importance of non verbal Communication
   a. People speak words for only 10 to 11 minutes daily. The standard spoken sentence takes 2.5 seconds.

b. In normal, two-person conversations, verbal components carry less than 35 percent of the social meaning; all the rest, 65 percent, is carried by non verbal components.

3. Non verbal Communication Is Continuous
   a. One cannot not communicate. Non verbal cues come continuously.
   b. We send and receive non verbal messages in an uninterrupted, persistent flow. And while we are observing someone else's gestures and mannerisms, that person may also be observing ours.

4. Non verbal Communication Conveys Emotions
   a. If we want to convey sincerity, our facial and bodily gestures can probably do it more effectively than our words, although words reinforced by non verbal cues will convey the most unmistakable message.
   b. Since non verbal cues are so closely tied to the emotions, how well we understand non verbal messages depends on how empathic we are.

5. Non verbal Communication is Rich in Meaning
   a. Iatrogenics is the study of how doctor-talk can intensify and even reduce or induce illness.
   b. The slightest sound or the most delicate movement can be fraught with meaning.

6. Non verbal Communication Can Be Confusing
   a. Certain cues can mean something entirely different from what we imagine.
   b. We must be careful in interpreting non verbal cues. We do not always have enough information to make a judgment, and our guesses may be far from accurate.

7. Do Your Actions Match Your Words?
   a. One of the best and most logical ways to check your interpretation of somebody's non verbal message is through that person's words.
   b. What you should watch for is whether the words and the actions are congruent. When there is congruency, you can be surer of your interpretations
      i. We try to get more information.
      ii. We suspend judgment.
      iii. We tend to believe either what we hear or what we see.
   c. Non verbal and verbal communication usually work together, even if incongruently:
      i. A non verbal message may repeat what we say, reinforcing it.
      ii. A non verbal message may replace verbal communication when we wave without saying "good-bye."
      iii. A non verbal message may underscore the verbal portion of a message in the way that italics strengthen the written word

     iv. A non verbal message may regulate behavior when we realize it is our turn to speak in a conversation as a result of a questioning look by another.

     v. A non verbal message may contradict the verbal message. When a person's actions and words contradict each other, we rely more on his or her actions to reveal true feelings.

8. Forms of Non verbal Communication

    Our non verbals of whatever kind, conscious or unconscious, may be characterized as follow:

    a. They always communicate something, "We cannot not communicate."

    b. They are believed.

    c. They are bound to the situation.

    d. They affect our relationships.

Since non verbal communication occupies a significant portion of human communication, it is worth exploring. Human communication refers to (1) the ways in which humans send messages to other humans, and (2) the correlation of the way in which humans receive messages from other humans. The process is a complex one. For example, an individual may be both the sender and receiver of the message (self-communication). Moreover, messages are mediated by or modified by the receiver's responses. And, finally, contradictory messages can be transmitted simultaneously.

Two major modes of human communication can be recognized: non verbal and verbal, or paralinguistic and linguistic.

1. Non verbal or paralinguistic communication

    Non verbal messages are those messages transmitted without the aid of language, or in conjunction with language. Non verbal messages may be more primitive (both phylogenetically and ontogenetically) than linguistic messages. As such, they carry much information about the emotional state of the sender. They are also richly larded with the cultural attributes of the sender. Finally, non verbal communication is continuous. Non verbally, you cannot not communicate. Some components of non verbal communications are:

    a. Organismics refers to the effect of the physical attributes of communication, particularly those physical attributes that are relatively unalterable: eye color, skin color, body dimensions, etc.

    b. Cosmetics refers to the effects of physical alterations (applicative and surgical) on communication.

    c. Costuming refers to the way dress affects communication.

    d. Proxemics refers the way space is used in communication.

e. Chronemics refers to the use of time in communication.
f. Oculesics refers to the use of eyes in communication.
g. Haptics refers to the use of touch to communicate feelings and emotions.
h. Kinesics refers to body movement in communication.
i. Objectics refers to both the use and choice of objects in communication.
j. Vocalics refers to the use and quality of the human voice in communication.

## SUGGESTED ACTIVITIES

### Vocalics

*Procedure*

Have each of the dyad sets (see Table 6.1) practice the vocal cues with the various roles. Allow the environment and individuals to affect vocal variation.

### Class Discussion

To what extent did the gender of the person enacting the role affect the vocal variation? To what extent did the gender of the role affect vocalics? Do women speak differently when they are talking to men than when they are talking to other women? Do men similarly change their vocal inflection when they are speaking to men or to women? How do these changes show themselves? What do these changes communicate to others? For instance, if a person who is speaking in a romantic setting typically uses a breathy, soft tone of voice and if men tend to use a breathy, soft tone of voice whenever they speak to women, what are men communicating? Try to recall specific examples of differences in vocal variation that seemed unusual to you. What did it communicate? Why did it seem unusual? Do you perceive differences in the way that women and men generally use vocal variation?

**Table 6.1.  Break the Class Into Dyads and Give Them the Following Set of Dialogue and Roles.**

| Dialogue: | Roles: |
|---|---|
| 1. Hi. | 1. Two people angry at each other. |
| 2. Having a good time? | 2. A teacher talking to a student. |
| 3. How are you doing? | 3. A friend talking to another friend who has just broken up a friendship. |
| 4. Let's get out of here. | 4. Two strangers who meet at a party. |
| 5. What's the matter? | 5. Two lovers talking at a candlelight dinner. |

## OCULESICS

### Functions of Eye Communication

To seek feedback
To inform the other person the channel of communication is open
To signal the nature of the relationship
To compensate for increased physical distance
Proxemics
Spatial Distances
Intimate
0–18 inches
Personal
1-1/2–4 feet
Social
4–12 feet
Public
12–25 feet
Invitation to Insight
Distance makes a difference

1. Choose a partner, and go to opposite sides of the room and face each other.
2. Very slowly begin walking toward each other while carrying on a conversation. You might simply talk about how you feel as you follow the activity. As you move closer, try to be aware of any change in your feelings. Continue moving slowly toward each other until you are only an inch or so apart. Remember how you feel at this point.
3. Now, while still facing each other, back up until you're at a comfortable distance for carrying on your conversation.
4. Share your feelings with each other and (or) with the whole group.

### Chronemics

*Time Questionnaire*

How long is it when someone says . . . (Answer in seconds, minutes, hours, days, years, centuries)

We're almost there.
A little while.
Just a second.
I've been waiting a long time.
Just a minute.

It took forever.
I've been waiting a long time.
I'll be back before you know it.
Let's think about this for a while.
It was ages ago.
I'll love you forever.

Do you like to be kept waiting? How long will you wait for or to . . . (Answer in seconds, minutes, hours, etc.)

A bus
A doctor
A job interview
A long-distance call
A local call
Buy tickets for a movie
Buy tickets for a concert
Get waited on at McDonald's
Register for classes

## Haptics

*Invitation to Insight*

**The Rules of Touch.**    Like most types of non verbal behavior, touching is governed by cultural and social rules. Imagine you are writing a guidebook for visitors from another culture. Describe the rules that govern touching in the following relationships. In each case, describe how the gender of the participants affects the rules.

   a. An adult and a 5-year-old-child
   b. An adult and a 12-year-old
   c. Two good friends
   d. Boss and employee

## Kinesics

*Body Exercises*

Facial expression practice:

1. Play checkers with a child of eleven; (s)he wins.
2. Hang a picture.

3. Listen to a radio broadcast (the news).
4. Unlock a padlock that is hard to open.
5. Read a book, refusing to be interrupted.

Arm-and-hand response:

1. Clean rings.
2. Count money.
3. Lift a heavy weight.
4. Sculpt a statue.
5. Sharpen a knife.
6. Sharpen a pencil.
7. Unlock a door.
8. Wind and set a watch.
9. Try on gloves.

Walking practice:

1. An art critic sauntering through an art gallery.
2. An important businessman stalking into his office.
3. A golfer tramping from tee to green on the golf course.
4. A tall man keeping step with a petite woman.
5. A woman threading her way across a crowded thoroughfare.
6. A person on a cruise pacing the deck of an ocean liner.
7. A delivery person staggering under a load.

The use of various art forms that involve body movement is now becoming functional. Dance artists, actors and singers are becoming centers of interest as people who know how to use movement for communicative purposes.

Edward T. Hall (1959), in his landmark commentary, The Silent Language, starts with his assumption that, "What people do is frequently more important than what they say." Hall's thesis is that every human culture is constructed on 10 primary message systems.

1. The Interactional system involves linguistic communication, vocalization, kinesics, and the like.
2. The Organizational system has to do with the social structure: class caste, and government.
3. The Economic System deals with work in maintenance occupations.
4. The Sexual Message System describes the biological, social and cultural relations between male and female.

5. The Territorial Message System concerns space, boundaries, formal and informal position relationships, places, property, and the like.
6. The Temporal Message System treats cultural activities such as teaching and learning, enculturation, education, and rearing children.
7. Instructional Message System deals with teaching and learning.
8. Recreational Primary Message System describes participation in the arts and sports, with entertainment, games, and fun.
9. The Protective Message System concerns protecting and being protected; formal, informal, and technical defenses; self-defense, and care of health.
10. The Exploitation Message System is a material system that allows human contact with the environment and involves the technology of equipment and materials in dealing with property and human behavior.

In his book, Sense Relaxation, Bernard Gunther (1986) describes non verbal communication as follows:

> Shaking hands, your posture, facial expressions, your appearance, voice tone, hair style, your clothes, the expression in your eyes, your smile, how close you stand to others, how you listen, your confidence, your breathing, the way you move, the way you stand, how you touch other people.

These aspects of you affect your relationship with other people, often without your and their realizing it. The body talks; its message is how you really are, not how you think you are.

## NON VERBAL BEHAVIOR

Charles Darwin, as early as 1872, wrote an essay, "The Expression of Emotions in Man and Animals." In that essay, he analyzed the expressions of emotions in man with examples from his own observations and reports and suggested that bodily expression is innate in the species. Since that time, much attention has been devoted to movement. Now researchers in many disciplines are studying non verbal communication.

The current interest seems to center on the intricacies of movement as it accompanies the spoken word and as it appears to be involved in interactions between persons. The effect of eyes upon dominance, anxiety, dependence, affection and the like, has commanded much attention.

Distance of persons from one another during the communication event has attracted a number of researchers, including anthropologists. Such matters as posture, facial expressions, scope and manner of movement, degrees of freedom and restriction of the movements and muscle tension are subjects of investigation.

## The Voice as a Non Verbal Cue

Voice usually reflects some of the speaker's inner reaction and attitude, can be controlled and developed to provide proper reinforcement for verbal messages.

Pitch: highness or lowness of voice tone

Quality: physical and emotional state of the speaker, clarity, resonance, vibrancy and richness, depends on the physical and emotional state of the speaker

## Volume-Loudness

*Rate and Rhythm*

***Physical activity as a non verbal cue.***   Movements of the body reinforce verbal messages or contradict them. Freeing the body from the conditioned restraints of bodily activity is one of the greatest problems in developing effective person-to-person speech communication.

Each person should develop his (or her) own mode of physical expression in respect to intent, the situation, context and nature of the message.

Bodily movements should develop from internal feeling associated with the message being transmitted.

## Identifying Feelings

*Purpose*

To determine how you deal with various feelings and emotions.

*Instructions*

Complete the "feelings" survey in Table 6.2 by circling the number which expresses how well you deal with each feeling listed.

1. Can express easily and completely in any situation
2. Can express most of the time

**Table 6.2.   Identifying Feelings**

| Caring | 1 | 2 | 3 | 4 | 5 | Love | 1 | 2 | 3 | 4 | 5 |
|---|---|---|---|---|---|---|---|---|---|---|---|
| Concern | 1 | 2 | 3 | 4 | 5 | Sadness | 1 | 2 | 3 | 4 | 5 |
| Depression | 1 | 2 | 3 | 4 | 5 | Fear | 1 | 2 | 3 | 4 | 5 |
| Anger | 1 | 2 | 3 | 4 | 5 | Tension | 1 | 2 | 3 | 4 | 5 |
| Disappointment | 1 | 2 | 3 | 4 | 5 | Hurt | 1 | 2 | 3 | 4 | 5 |
| Excitement | 1 | 2 | 3 | 4 | 5 | Pride | 1 | 2 | 3 | 4 | 5 |

3. Can express some of the time—with difficulty
4. Can express rarely—with reservation
5. Cannot express this emotion

Complete the following sentences:

1. I very much care about
2. The thing which depresses me most frequently is
3. I feel tense when
4. The thing that hurts me most is
5. I am excited about
6. I take pride in
7. I am disappointed with
8. The thing that frightens me most is
9. I get angry when
10. I am concerned about
11. I feel sad when
12. Love is a feeling

## How I Express My Feelings

*Purpose*

To identify how you personally express a variety of emotions or feelings.

*Instructions*

Being as spontaneous as possible, complete the following sentences:

1. When I'm angry, I express it by
2. When I'm worried, I express it by
3. When I'm sad, I express it by
4. When I'm depressed, I express it by
5. When I feel like a failure, I express it by
6. When I'm afraid, I express it by
7. When I feel successful, I express it by
8. When I feel affectionate, I express it by
9. When I feel guilty, I express it by
10. When I feel lonely, I express it by
11. When I feel hurt, I express it by
12. When I feel rejected, I express it by

Emotions: our feelings

*happiness, sadness, depression, joy*

Emotional Expression: the way we choose to communicate our feelings

*talking about it, fighting, refusing to speak, throwing things, clinging*

Emotional Behavior: the way we act out the emotions we feel

*Acting angrily or acting calmly*

*Acting lovesick or acting calmly*

## GUIDELINES FOR EMOTIONAL EXPRESSION

1. Communication is irreversible.
2. Express emotions tentatively.
3. Feelings change rapidly.
4. Use I-messages.
5. All behavior communicates.
6. Verbalize your feelings.
7. Use non-obvious situations to express emotions.

## DESCRIBING EMOTIONS

1. Don't evaluate emotions; just describe them.
2. Describe the intensity of the emotion.
3. Own your own feelings.
4. Describe what influenced you to feel as you do.
5. Describe what you want the listener to do.

# Chapter Seven

# Listening

Listening is like physical exercise. Everyone knows it is important, but many may find it difficult to do on a regular basis. Listening is hard work. Thomas and Sherblom (2006) tell us the reason why listening is difficult is physiological in origin. Too often we allow ourselves to be distracted. These distractions may be physical (a hot room, uncomfortable clothing, loud noises, or allowing preconceived attitudes to prematurely determine the value of what the other person is saying. An important principle of communication is to listen and respond thoughtfully to others. Listening is the process of making sense out of what we hear. Listening is an active process of receiving, processing, and interpreting aural stimuli. Firstly, listening involves taking in meaningful sounds and noises and in some way, retraining and using them. Just as we speak for different purposes, we also listen for different purposes. We listen for enjoyment, information and evaluation.

Listening is part of the transactional process of communication. The receiver's responses have a direct impact on the direction of the conversation. The key is to become active listeners rather than passive ones. Active listening involves providing feedback that clarifies and extends a speaker's message.

A step in improving listening abilities is to recognize and combat the various obstacles to listening. They are preoccupation with self, preoccupation with external issues, such as leveling, and learning what is expected.

You can help yourself remember what is said by using three organizing techniques: chunking, ordering, and reordering. Chunking is the grouping of bits of information according to a mutual relationship. Ordering is the arranging of bits of information into a systematic sequence. Reordering is the changing of an existing system or organizing information so that a new or different sequence is developed.

Empathic listening is listening to understand another person's message from his or her point of view. It requires attention to both the content and the feeling of the message. One must establish rapport, communicate acceptance, and encourage the speaker to continue talking. Empathic listening requires an understanding of the basic helping process model: Involving, Exploring, Resolving, Concluding. To be a good empathic listener, one should restate what is said and use verbal and nonverbal feedback to show that you understand.

## LISTENING BEHAVIORS

How frequently do you find yourself engaging in each of the following listening behaviors? On the line, indicate 5 for frequently, 4 for often, 3 for sometimes, 2 for rarely, and 1 for never.

1. I listen differently, depending on whether I am listening for enjoyment, understanding, or evaluation.
2. I stop listening when what the person is saying to me isn't interesting to me.
3. I consciously try to recognize the speaker's purpose.
4. I pretend to listen to people when I am really thinking about other things.
5. When people talk, I differentiate between their main points and supporting details.
6. When the person's manner of speaking annoys me (such as muttering, stammering, or talking in a monotone), I stop listening carefully.
7. At various places in a conversation, I paraphrase what the speaker said in order to check my understanding.
8. When I perceive the subject matter as very difficult, I stop listening carefully.
9. When the person is presenting detailed information, I take good notes of major points and supporting details.
10. When people use words that I find offensive, I stop listening and start preparing responses.

SCORING THE SURVEY: In this list, the even-numbered items indicate negative listening behaviors, so to score yourself, you need to reverse the scoring of these items. If you gave yourself 5, count it as 1, 4 count it as 2, 3 count it as 3, 2 count it as 4, 1 count it as 5. The odd-numbered items indicate positive listening behaviors. Count each as given. Sum all your scores. There are 50 points possible. If you score over 40, you are effective in your listening. If you score below 40, identify the questions that seemed to cause your lowest scores. You will want to give particular attention to the sections of this chapter that relate to these areas.

"Listen, my children. . ."
"Hearing is one of the body's five senses. But listening is an art."

—Frank Tyger

"We have been given two ears and but a single mouth, in order that we may hear more and talk less."

—Zeno of Citium

"Hear twice before you speak once."

—Scottish saying

"Bore: one who talks when you wish they would listen.

—Ambrose Bierce

## What Listening Isn't

Listening isn't just hearing.
Listening isn't automatic.
Listening isn't passive.

## What Listening Is

Listening is active.
Listening is paying attention.
Listening is understanding.
Listening is evaluating.
Listening is interpreting.

## What is Listening?

Listening is an active process of receiving, processing, and interpreting aural stimuli.

## Why Do We Listen?

To become a better listener, consider three simple processes: stop, look and listen as we listen.

1. For enjoyment
2. For information
3. To help
4. For evaluation

Becoming a more effective listener is an exciting and rewarding experience. Listening is a process that includes hearing, attending, and understanding, evaluating, and responding to spoken messages. Listening requires effort, motivation, and knowledge.

Four specific benefits of listening:

1. Increased knowledge
2. Job success
3. Improved interpersonal relations
4. Self-protection

Increased knowledge: The world is filled with information to be consumed through listening. Electronic Age-people will need to use listening more, not less, in the future.

Job success: Increasingly, employers are looking for people who have oral communication skills. Listening affects the understanding of a problem, the retention and attention of an individual, and the morale of a group.

Improved Interpersonal relations: Effective listening is important not only when you are in formal situations and job settings, but also when you interact informally with friends, room mates, spouses, colleagues, etc. Listening skills help initiate and maintain important relationships.

Self-Protection: Edmund Burke (1968), "All that is necessary for the forces of evil to win the world is for enough good men to do nothing. In a free society, there can be only the most limited legal restrictions on the freedom to speak."

## ROADBLOCKS TO COMMUNICATION

While the following statements might be used in some cases, they inhibit effective listening. Covey (1989) identifies one good listening habit: "Seek first to understand, and only then be understood" Effective listeners place understanding the other person first. The following responses illustrate some statements which do not necessarily demonstrate effective listening.

### Typical Responses

1. ORDERING, DIRECTING, COMMANDING (You must . . . .," "you have to . . . .," "You will . . .")
2. WARNING, ADMONISHING, THREATENING ("You had better . . . .," "If you don't, then. . . ")

3. MORALIZING, PREACHING, OBLIGING ("You should . . .," "You ought to . . .," "It is your duty . . .," "It is your responsibility . . .," ""You are required. . .")

4. ADVISING, GIVING SUGGESTIONS OR SOLUTIONS ("What I would do is . . .," "Why don't you . . .," "Let me suggest . . .," "It would be best for you. . .")

5. PERSUADING WITH LOGIC, ARGUING, INSTRUCTING, And LECTURING ("Do you realize . . .," "Here is why you are wrong . . .," "That is not right . . ., the facts are . . .," "Yes, but. . .")

6. JUDGING, CRITICIZING, DISAGREEING, BLAMING ("You are bad," "You are lazy," "You are not thinking straight," "You are acting foolishly," "Your hair is too long".)

7. PRAISING, AGREEING, EVALUATING POSITIVELY, APPROVING ("You're a good boy," "You've done a good job," "That's a nice thing to do")"

8. NAME-CALLING, RIDICULING, SHAMING ("You're a spoiled brat," "Stupid," Crybaby," Okay, Mr. Smarty")

9. INTERPRETING, ANALYZING, DIAGNOSING ("What you need is . . .," "What's wrong with you is . . .," "You're just trying to get attention . . .," "You don't really mean that," "Your problem is. . .")

10. REASSURING, SYMPATHIZING, CONSOLING, SUPPORTING ("It's not so bad . . .," "Don't worry," "You'll feel better," "That's too bad.")

11. PROBING, QUESTIONING, INTERROGATING ("Why . . .," "Who . . .," "Where . . .," "What . . .," "How . . .,")

12. WITHDRAWING, DISTRACTING, HUMORING, DIVERTING ("We don't talk about that at the dinner table," "That reminds me." "Get up on the wrong side of bed?")

13. INTERRUPTING breaks the flow of communication

14. PROLONGED SILENCE (" ")

Source: Stephanie Schaeffer

There are six forms of non listening.

1. Pseudo listening is pretending to be attentive to what another or others are saying.

2. Monopolizing occurs when a person hogs the conversational stage.

3. Selective listening involves either selectively focusing on parts of communication that support our views and that interest us or selectively screening out parts of communication that diverge from our view or that do not interest us.

4. Defensive listening occurs when individuals interpret what others say in a protective, apprehensive manner.
5. Ambushing is listening for the purpose of attacking the person speaking and (or) that person's ideas.
6. Literal listening occurs when individuals attend only to the content-level of meaning in communication and overlook the relational level of meaning.

## SKILLS TO ENCOURAGE COMMUNICATION

Silence
Acknowledge
Door Openers
Feedback Skills:
    Parroting (repeating)
    Paraphrasing, Summarizing
Actively Listening Empathically:
Picking up on the underlying feeling

## SUGGESTED ACTIVITIES

### Empathic Listening

*Objective*

To develop skills of empathy in communication by active and effective listening.

Select a topic of a controversial nature from a magazine or local newspaper. Subjects could be politics, labor, management, or any other topic in good taste. Subdivide participants into groups of three. Each triad selects a Speaker, Listener, and Referee. The selected topic is discussed by the Speaker, who, without interruption, explains his or her feelings on that topic. After the Speaker has finished, the Listener summarizes (without notes) what was said on the subject. Following this segment, Speaker and Referee can correct or amplify any item stated by the Listener. The Referee is the only person allowed to use notes. After an eight-ten minute discussion, select a new topic and reverse roles, using the same procedure. After eight-ten minutes, another new topic and role reversals are used, thus allowing each person to act in each of the three roles.

**Table 7.1. Suggestions about Listening Habits**

| *Bad Listening Habits* | *Good Listening Habits* |
|---|---|
| Calling subject "uninteresting." | Tuning in the speaker to see if there is anything you can use. |
| Criticizing speaker's delivery, personal appearance, etc. | Getting the speaker's message which is probably more important. |
| Getting overexcited and preparing rebuttal. | Hearing the person out before you judge her. |
| Listening only for facts. | Listening also for main ideas, principles and concepts. |
| Trying to make an outline of everything. | Listening a couple of minutes before taking notes. |
| Faking attention to the speaker. | Good listening is not totally relaxed. There is a collection of tensions inside. |
| Tolerating distractions. | Doing something about the distractions, closing a door, requesting a person to speak louder, etc. |
| Avoiding difficult material | Learning to listen to difficult material. |
| Letting emotion-laden words affect listening. | Trying to understand your reaction to emotion-laden words which might cause barriers. |
| Wasting difference between speech speed (words per minute) and thought speed (words per minute). | Making thought speed an asset instead of a liability by:<br>a. anticipating the next point to be made.<br>b. mentally summarizing. |

Ralph Nichols and Leonard Stevens, *Are You Listening?*

*Discussion Questions*

1. In your role as Speaker, did you sense any difficulties or experience any awkward moments?
2. How about as Listener or Referee?
3. Did you identify or observe any barriers that obstructed effective listening?
4. In your role as Listener, why was it difficult to summarize and paraphrase the Speaker's comments?

*Materials*

Newspaper or magazine articles, as needed.

*Approximate Time Required*

Twenty-Thirty Minutes

*Source*

Unknown
  Effective listening is adapted to specific communication goals.

1. Informational and critical listening require mindfulness, efforts to control obstacles, asking questions, using aids to recall, and organizing information.
2. Relational listening requires mindfulness, suspending judgment, understanding the other's perspective (dual perspective), and expressing support.
3. Other listening purposes are to experience pleasure and to discriminate.

## Communicating Feelings

*Objectives*

At the end of this session, students should be able to:

1. Relate how emotions are communicated.
2. Develop the ability to identify the emotional tone of a message.
3. Demonstrate the practice of active (empathic) listening.

*Procedure*

Read the following statements to the class, and ask students to identify the underlying feeling expressed by the content of the message.

1. "I shouldn't have failed this test! I studied all night for it!" (amazed, shocked)
2. "Why did we start playing this game? It's taking much longer to finish than I thought it would." (bored)
3. "The candy is delicious. It was so nice of you to bring it" (pleased)
4. "I can't talk to my advisor alone. Will you go with me?" (afraid)
5. "Ever since my roommate got a new car, all he or she has being doing is going out!" (envious)
6. "Don't come near me. You don't care about anyone but yourself!" (hurt)
7. "That jerk just ran a stoplight!" (angry)
8. "I'm sorry about what I said about your friend. I shouldn't have said anything" (guilty)
9. "How fun to go out for dinner for a change!" (excited)
10. "What do you mean we can't go to a movie tonight?" (confused)

## LISTENING FOR TOTAL MEANING

Listen to all levels of a message:

1. Listen to both verbal and non verbal messages.
2. Listen to what speakers omit.
3. Listen for both content and relationship messages.
4. Confront mixed messages in a non-threatening way.

    Supportive Listening
    Listening with a view toward
    Understanding
    Keeping an open mind
    Avoiding filtering out
    Undesirable messages
    Recognizing your own biases
    Invitation to Insight

## What Would You Do?

1. In a moment you'll read a list of situations in which someone tells you of a problem. In each case, write out the words you'd use in responding to this person.
2. Here are the statements:
    a. I don't know what to do about my parents. It seems as if they just don't understand me. Everything I like seems to go against their values, and they just won't accept my feelings as being right for me. It's not that they don't love me. They do, but they don't accept me.
    b. I've been pretty discouraged lately. I just can't get a good relationship going with any guys . . . I mean a romantic relationship. . . . You know. I have plenty of men whom I'm good friends with, but that's always as far as it goes. I'm tired of being just a pal. . . . I want to be more than that.
    c. (Child to parents) I hate you guys! You always go out and leave me with some stupid sitter. Why don't you like me?
    d. I'm really bummed out. I don't know what I want to do with my life. I'm pretty tired of school, but there aren't any good jobs around, and I sure don't want to join the service. I could just drop out for a while, but that doesn't really sound very good either.
    e. Things really seem to be kind of lousy in my marriage lately. It's not that we fight too much or anything, but all the excitement seems to be gone. It's like we're in a rut, and it keeps getting worse. . . .

f. I keep getting the idea that my boss is angry with me. It seems as if lately he hasn't been joking around very much, and he hasn't said anything at all about my work for about three weeks now. I wonder what I should do.

3. Once you've written your response to each of these messages, imagine the probable outcome of the conversation that would have followed. If you've tried this exercise in class, you might have two group members role-play each statement. Based on your idea of how the conversation might have gone, decide which responses were helpful and which were unproductive.

## Possible Topics for Listening

In groups of three, one person would choose a topic and be the speaker; another would be the listener and paraphrase the words of the speaker, and the third would be a referee. After one round, participants should switch roles.

1. Describe an experience of being in love.
2. What are some effective studying techniques?
3. What is the wisest or most profound thing you have ever learned?
4. Describe what it feels like to be lonely.
5. What are the most important qualities in physical attractiveness?
6. What would be the ideal student-teacher relationship?
7. Describe an example of bias or prejudice that you have witnessed or experienced.
8. Where are the best places to go to meet new people?
9. What are the qualities that *outstanding* teachers possess?
10. Describe an experience where you came across as a complete failure.
11. What is it that *most* motivates you in the classroom?
12. What are some specific topics people discuss when they first meet each other?
13. Describe, as clearly as you can, your fundamental, or root values.
14. What do you think of sex-role stereotyping in our society?
15. What are some changes you would like to see in our society?
16. Describe what death and dying mean to you.
17. What are the qualities that most make you want to listen to someone else?
18. What are the times or circumstances where cheating is justified?
19. Describe what it's like to experience and enjoy nature.
20. What are the best qualities of a true friend?
21. If you could accomplish anything, what would you most like to accomplish in your lifetime?
22. Describe the scariest nightmare you have ever had.

23. What does it take to be a well-organized person?
24. What suggestions would you make to a chronic procrastinator?
25. Describe what it's like to have a loving, intimate relationship.
26. What are those things in your life of which you are most proud?
27. What kinds of things should a person with a short temper do to control their anger?
28. Describe what it was like being brought up in your family.
29. Given total freedom, what kind of lifestyle would you like to have?
30. What do you think is the *ideal* personality trait to possess?
31. What would you suggest is the greatest shortcoming of today's generation?
32. On what issue have you taken your most recent public stand? Or shared a specific viewpoint on an issue with someone else?
33. Describe how it feels to be a winner, or to be successful.
34. What is something that has really disturbed you lately?
35. What would you like to be doing ten or twenty years from now?
36. Describe what it's like to perform or speak before a large audience.
37. What is one thing you have never tried but would like to?
38. What are the qualities necessary for a successful relationship?
39. Describe something you have seen or experienced that has made a deep and long-lasting impression on you.
40. What suggestions would you give to someone who wanted to become a fascinating person?
41. What suggestions would you give to someone who was just starting college?
42. Describe what you think the *ideal* educational environment would be.
43. If you had your life to live over, what one thing would you change?

*Chapter Eight*

# Interviewing

An interview is a communication transaction that emphasizes questions and answers (Lumsden and Lumsden, 1997). The word interview suggests a sharing of views in which the interviewer and interviewee are involved, and listening and speaking are equally important.

You will no doubt find yourself in a wide variety of interviewing situations throughout your social and professional life. As you will see throughout this chapter, your effectiveness whether as interviewer or interviewee in this form of communication will prove crucial in helping you achieve many of your goals. Interviewing includes a wide range of communication situations:

- A supervisor evaluates a trainee.
- A salesperson tries to sell a client a new car.
- A teacher advises a student about graduate schools.
- A counselor talks with a family about their communication problems.
- A recent graduate applies to Microsoft for a job in the product development division.
- A building owner questions a potential apartment renter.
- A lawyer examines a witness during a trial.
- An employer discusses some of the reasons for terminating a contract with a consultant.
- A boss offers a performance review to an employee and invites the employee's feedback.

## INTERVIEWING DEFINED

Interviewing is a form of interpersonal communication in which two people interact most often face-to-face, largely through a question-and-answer format to achieve specific goals. While interviews usually involve two people, some involve more. At job fairs, for example, where many people apply for the same few jobs, interviewers may talk with several persons at once. Similarly, counseling interviews frequently involve entire families, groups of co-workers, or other related individuals.

Although most interviewing is done face-to-face, much interviewing is now taking place via computer through e-mail and on Internet Relay Chat groups. For example, you can use e-mail or IRC groups to conduct an informative interview with people living in different parts of the world. The Internet enables employers to interview candidates in different parts of the world all for the price of a few local phone calls. Of course, it enables candidates to explore employment opportunities from their own desks. With advanced hardware and software enabling audio and video exchanges over the Internet, the computer-mediated interview will very closely resemble the traditional, face-to-face situation.

The interview is different from other forms of communication because it proceeds through questions and answers. Both parties in the interview can ask and answer questions, but most often the interviewer asks and the interviewee answers. The specific goals of the interview guide and structure its content and format. In an employment interview, for example, the interviewer's goal is to find an applicant who can fulfill the tasks of the position. The interviewee's goal is to get the job, if it seems desirable.

Interviews vary from relatively informal talks that resemble everyday conversations to those with rigidly prescribed questions in a set order. Select the interview structure that best fits your specific purpose, or combine the various types to create a new interview structure tailored to your needs

- The informal interview resembles conversation; the general theme is chosen in advance, but the specific questions arise from the context. This type of interview is especially useful for obtaining information informally.
- The guided interview deals with topics chosen in advance. The specific questions and wordings, however, are guided by the ongoing interaction. It is useful in assuring maximum flexibility and responsiveness to the dynamics of the situation. The interviews on television talk shows are good examples of this format.
- The standard open interview relies on open-ended questions with their order selected in advance. It is useful when standardization is needed, for example, when interviewing several candidates for the same job.
- The quantitative interview uses questions that guide responses into pre-established categories. For example, questions may contain multiple choice responses that the interviewee would select from or may ask for a number from 1 to 10 to indicate an interviewee's level of agreement. It is useful when large amounts of information (which can be put into categories) are

to be collected and statistically analyzed, for example, in a market survey of customer satisfaction.

We can also distinguish the different types of interviews by the goals of the interviewer and interviewee. Some of the most important interviews are persuasion, appraisal, exit, counseling, information and employment. You will probably come into contact most often with information and employment interviews, so these are covered in detail. The discussion of the information interview focuses on the role of the interviewer, and the employment interview discussion, on the role of the interviewee, roles you are most likely to experience now and in the near future. Of course, the principles for effective information and employment interviews will also prove useful for other types of interviews.

## THE PERSUASION INTERVIEW

The goal of the persuasion interview is to change a person's attitudes, beliefs, or behaviors. One way in which this is accomplished is for the interviewer to ask questions that will lead to the desired conclusion. For example, if you go into a showroom to buy a new car, the salesperson may ask you questions that are obviously and favorably answered by the car he or she wants to sell; for example, "Is safety an important factor?" or "Do you want to save a bundle?" Another way is for the salesperson to become the interviewee, explaining the superiority of this car above all others in answer to your questions about mileage, safety features, and finance terms.

All interviews contain elements of both information and persuasion. When, for example, a guest appears on *The Tonight Show* and talks about a new movie, information is communicated. There is also persuasion; the performer is trying to persuade the audience to see the movie.

## THE APPRAISAL INTERVIEW

In the evaluation or appraisal interview, the interviewee's job performance is assessed by his or her supervisor, management, or colleagues on the work team. The general aim is to communicate what the interviewee is doing well, offer praise and encouragement, as well as to identify what needs improvement, the reasons for this, and to develop a plan to improve performance. These interviews are important because they help all members of an organization see how their performances match the expectations of those making promotion and firing decisions. These interviews also help teach employees the norms and rules of the organizational culture; they spell out what it takes to succeed in the company.

## THE EXIT INTERVIEW

The exit interview is used widely by organizations in the United States and throughout the world. When an employee leaves a company voluntarily, it is important for management to know why. All organizations compete for superior employees; if an organization is losing them, it must discover why, to prevent others from leaving. This type of interview also provides a method for making the departure as pleasant and efficient as possible for both employee and employer.

## THE COUNSELING INTERVIEW

Counseling interviews provide guidance. The goal is to help the person deal more effectively with problems involving work, friends or lovers, or just the hassles of daily living. For the interview to be of any value, the interviewer must learn about the person's habits, problems, self-perceptions, goals, and so on. With this information, the counselor tries to persuade the person to alter certain aspects of his or her thinking or behaving. The counselor may try to persuade you, for example, to listen more attentively to relationship messages or to devote more time to your class work.

## THE INFORMATION INTERVIEW

In the information interview, the interviewer tries to learn something about the interviewee, usually a person of some reputation and accomplishment. The interviewer asks the interviewee a series of questions designed to elicit his or her views, beliefs, insights, perspective, predictions, life history, and so on. Examples of the information interview are those published in popular magazines and newspapers. The television interviews conducted by Conan O'Brien, Rosie O'Donnell, Larry King, and Diane Sawyer, as well as many of those conducted by lawyers during a trial, are all information interviews. Each aims to gather specific information from someone who supposedly knows something others do not.

Information interviews are commonly used to gather information about a specific career field and to evaluate employment opportunities. Let us say that you are conducting an interview to get information about the available job opportunities, and the preparation you will need to get into desktop publishing. Here are a few guidelines for conducting such an information-gathering interview:

## SECURE AN APPOINTMENT

In selecting a person to interview, you might, for example, look through your college catalog for a desktop publishing course and interview the instructor, or you might call a local publishing company and ask for the person in charge of desktop publishing. Try to learn something about the person before the interview. For example, has the instructor written a book or articles about the field? Look at the book catalog, at indexes to periodicals, and at relevant websites.

Call or send a letter to request an interview and to identify the purpose of your request. For example, you might say, "I'm considering a career in desktop publishing, and I would appreciate an interview with you to learn more about the business and your company. The interview should take about 20 to 30 minutes." By stating up front a limited time for the interview, you make the interviewee know that it will not take too long. Since you are asking the favor of the interviewee's time, it is best to be available at her or his convenience. Indicate flexibility on your part, for example, "What time is good for you? I'm available any day next week after 12 noon."

If you find it necessary to conduct the interview by phone, call to set up a time for a future call. For example, you might say, "I'm interested in a career in desktop publishing, and I would like to interview you about job opportunities. If you agree, I can call you back at a time that's convenient for you." In this way, you don't run the risk of interrupting the interviewee's busy day and asking the person to hold still for an interview.

## PREPARE YOUR QUESTIONS

Preparing questions in advance will ensure using the time available to your best advantage. Of course, as the interview progresses, you may think of other questions, and you should pursue these, as well. A prepared list of questions that can be altered as the interview progresses will help you obtain efficiently the information you need.

Use open-ended questions that give the interviewee room to discuss the issues you want to raise. Instead of asking a question that asks for only a simple "yes" or "no", such as, "Do you have academic training in desktop publishing?" Ask open-ended questions that allow the person greater freedom to elaborate, such as, "Can you tell me about your background in this field?"

### Establish Rapport with the Interviewer

Open the interview by thanking the person for making the time available and again stating your interest in the field and the opportunity to learn more about it. Many people receive numerous requests, and it helps to remind the person of your specific purpose. You might say something like, "I really appreciate your making time for this interview. As I mentioned, I'm interested in learning about job opportunities in desktop publishing and learning about your experience in this are will help a great deal."

## ASK PERMISSION TO TAPE THE INTERVIEW

Generally, it is a good idea to tape record the interview. It will ensure accuracy and will also allow you to concentrate on the interviewee, rather than on note-taking. However, always ask for permission first. Even if the interview is being conducted by phone, ask permission if you intend to tape the conversation.

## CLOSE AND FOLLOW UP THE INTERVIEW

At the end of the interview, thank the person for making the time available, for being informative, cooperative, and helpful. Closing the interview on a positive note makes it easier to secure a second interview should you need it. Within the next two or three days, follow up the interview with a brief note of thanks.

## INFORMATIVE INTERVIEW

The questions below can be used for interviewer and interviewee to practice getting acquainted before they conduct the actual class interview.

### Childhood and Family

1. What characteristics did you have as a child that have remained?
2. What characteristics have you lost or changed on reaching adulthood?
3. What event or circumstances of your childhood do you think had the most impact on who you are right now?
4. Have you ever deliberately lied about a serious matter to either parent?
5. What were you most punished or criticized for when you were a child?

### Experiences and Philosophy

1. What experience or accomplishment has brought you the greatest amount of pride?
2. How do you feel about couples living together without being married?
3. Are females equal, inferior, or superior to males?

4. Have you ever been tempted to kill yourself?
5. How do you feel about crying in the presence of others?
6. Do you think there are times when cheating is justified?
7. How important is money to you?
8. Have you ever had a mystical experience?
9. Have you ever been arrested or fined for violating any law?

## Personality

1. Is there anything you sometimes pretend to be that you are not?
2. How loving a person are you? Give an example of something that you think shows how loving you are. (How would you rate yourself [loving wise] on a scale of 1–10?)
3. Have you ever disliked anyone to the extent of plotting things against them? (Explain the situation or circumstances.)
4. How honest are you? Rate yourself and give an example.
5. How attractive do you think you are? Rate and give example.
6. What are you most intellectual about?
7. What are you most emotional about?
8. What do you regard as your chief fault in personality?
9. What emotions do you find most difficult to control?

## Feedback

1. Name something you think I hate to do.
2. If you had just one word to describe me, what would it be?
3. What about me do you like the most?
4. To what person are you responding the most and how?

## Time

1. If you had just one year to live, and no financial restrictions, how would you like to spend the year?
2. If you had just one hour to live, starting right now, what would you want to do?
3. If you had just one minute to live, what would you like to say to me?

## Finish the Sentence

1. When I think about the future, I see myself . . .
2. When I am feeling anxious in a new situation, I usually . . .

3. The thing that turns me on the most is . . .
4. When I am rejected, I usually . . .
5. Breaking rules that seem arbitrary makes me feel . . .
6. I feel most affectionate when . . .
7. When I am alone, I usually . . .
8. I am rebellious when . . .
9. The emotion I find most difficult to control is . . .
10. I am afraid of . . .
11. I am most ashamed of . . .
12. One thing I'd like to improve in the way I start conversations is . . .
13. My biggest fear in meeting people is . . .
14. Would you help me with . . . ?
15. One thing I want you to know abut me is . . .

## EMPLOYMENT INTERVIEWING

Employment interviews allow employers and job candidates to assess each other and determine whether there is a good fit between them. Typically, employment interviews include periods of information giving and information getting, as well as persuasive efforts on the part of both participants. The prospective employer wants to convince the job candidate of the quality of the company, and the candidate wants to convince the prospective employer of the quality of his or her qualifications.

### Can You Identify Unlawful Questions?

Instructions: For each question write L (Lawful) if you think the question is legal for a interviewer to ask in an employment interview and U (Unlawful) if you think the question is illegal. For each question you consider unlawful, indicate why you think it is so classified.

1. Are you married, Tom?
2. When did you graduate from high school, Mary?
3. Do you have a picture so I can attach it to your resume?
4. Will you need to be near a mosque (church, synagogue)?
5. I see you taught courses in "gay and lesbian studies." Are you gay?
6. Is Chinese your native language?
7. Will you have difficulty getting a baby-sitter?
8. I notice that you walk with a limp. Is this a permanent injury?
9. Where were you born?
10. Have you ever been arrested for a crime?

Thinking critically about the legality of employment interview questions, all 10 questions are unlawful. Review the questions and try to identify the general principles of the illegality of employment interview questions. Think about how you would respond to each question if you were asked this in an actual job interview.

**Table 8.1.   Some Dos and Don'ts for Communicating in the Interview. These Dos and Don'ts are Organized Around the Qualities of Effective Communication. What Other Dos and Don'ts Would you Suggest Job Interviewees Observe?**

| Characteristic | Do | Don't |
|---|---|---|
| Openness | Answer questions as fully as appropriate. Give enough detail to answer the question | Give one-word answers that may signal a lack of interest or knowledge or at the other extreme, ramble or go off on tangents. |
| Empathy | See the questions from the interviewer's point of view. Focus your eye contact and orient your body toward the interviewer. Lean forward as appropriate. | Focus your attention away from the interviewer or the interview situation |
| Positiveness | Emphasize your positive qualities and your interest in the position and in the company. | Criticize yourself or emphasize your negative qualities. Criticize your previous employer or your education. |
| Immediacy | Connect yourself with the interviewer throughout the interview by, for example, using the interviewer's name, focusing clearly on the interviewer's remarks, and expressing responsibility for your thoughts and feelings. | Distance yourself from the interviewer, forget the interviewer's name (or mispronounce it), or fail to respond directly to the interviewer's questions. |
| Interaction Management | Ensure the interviewer's satisfaction by being positive, complimentary, and generally cooperative. | Appear defensive, cocky, lacking in assertiveness, extremely introverted, or overly aggressive. |
| Expressiveness | Let your nonverbal behaviors (especially facial expression and vocal variety) reflect your verbal messages and your general enthusiasm. | Fidget, move about excessively, or use self-adaptors, self-touching gestures that communicate a lack of confidence and comfort. Talk in a monotone or look bored or unenthusiastic |
| Other-Orientation | Focus on and express interest in the interviewer and the company. Express agreement and ask for clarification as appropriate. | Argue or engage in unnecessary criticism. |

## THE APPLICATION

Filling out an employment application is part of your interview. Usually, an interviewer sees your written application before they actually see you. Always:

1. Write clearly and neatly.
2. Be specific about position applied for.
3. Be accurate with dates and descriptions.
4. Fill in all blanks. If questions do not apply, write N/A.
5. Attach an updated resume. Be sure that application dates and resume dates match.

## WHAT TO WEAR

It is not necessary to feel you must spend very much money on interviewing clothes. If you are neat and clean and have put thought into your appearance, this will be reflected in your first impression. Taking the time to ensure a positive presentation of one's self assures the interviewer that you have enough respect for, and desire to be employed by, the company that you have taken the extra time to prepare.

## BEFORE THE INTERVIEW

Your interview begins the moment you leave your house. Helpful hints to make the interviewing process run more smoothly.

1. Act professionally as soon as you enter company premises. This includes:
   a. Not parking in reserved or handicapped spots.
   b. Not closing the front door in another person's face.
   c. Not fighting for a parking space.
   d. Not being rude to the receptionist.
2. Don't smoke or drink before your interview. You may think no one can smell it, but they do!

Table 8.2.    What to Wear; Dos and Don'ts

| Don't | Do |
| --- | --- |
| -Dress sloppy or creatively | -Wear a tie |
| -Wear an earring (men) | -Wear pantyhose (even in summer) |
| -Wear more than one pair of earrings (women) | -Dress conservatively |
| -Wear perfume or aftershave | -Keep hair out of eyes. |

3. Do your homework.
    a. What does the company do?
    b. What are the job requirements?
4. Be prepared to:
    a. Explain employment gaps
    b. Honestly account for your time.

**Table 8.3.  During and After the Interview**

| During | |
|---|---|
| *Don't* | *Do* |
| -Appear over confident or cocky | -Maintain eye contact |
| -Fidget | -Sit up straight |
| -Play with hair | -Offer a firm handshake |
| -Act casual | -Pay attention to surroundings |
| -Act bored, leaning back in chair | -Smile |
| *Don't* | *Do* |
| -Ramble | -Listen to questions asked |
| -Exaggerate experience | -Be specific and give examples |
| -Hedge on questions | -Accept responsibility for previous actions |
| -Ask about other applicants | -Be honest |
| | -Ask questions about the job (this shows interest |
| | -Ask for the job |
| *After the Interview* | |
| *Don't* | *Do* |
| -Call daily, hourly. Give the recruiter an opportunity to return your call. | -Send a handwritten thank-you note to everyone who interviewed you. (Be sure names and titles are correct.) -After a couple of days, you may want to follow up with a call. |

# Chapter Nine

# Interpersonal Communication

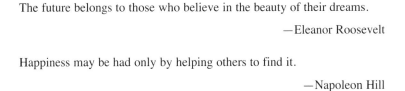

The future belongs to those who believe in the beauty of their dreams.

—Eleanor Roosevelt

Happiness may be had only by helping others to find it.

—Napoleon Hill

Interpersonal communication is a special form of unmediated human communication that occurs when we interact simultaneously with another person and attempt to mutually influence each other, usually for the purpose of managing relationships. To manage relationships, interpersonal communication involves quality. Interpersonal communication occurs not just when we interact with someone, but when we treat the other as a unique human being. Interpersonal communication occurs simultaneously. It's not a linear process but is a process in which both individuals simultaneously affect each other. Interpersonal communication involves mutual influence. Every interpersonal communication interaction influences us. Sometimes it changes our lives dramatically, sometimes in small ways. Long lasting interpersonal relationships are sustained not by one person giving and another taking, but by mutually satisfying communication that helps to manage relationships.

The process of interpersonal communication consists of elements that interact through mutual verbal interaction to produce the ongoing formation of norms as part of the process. On the simplest level, relationships are associations or connections between two or more people who are interdependent, who use consistent pattern of interactions, and have interacted for some period of time.

The better one understands the interpersonal communication process, the more likely they will create satisfying, productive and meaningful interpersonal relationships.

Interpersonal communication deals with communication between people. In one sense, all communication is between people; so all communication is interpersonal. Such a broad definition, however, doesn't create any useful boundaries for the area of study. Interpersonal communication is a special form of unmediated human communication that occurs when we interact simultaneously with another person and attempt to mutually influence each other, usually for the purpose of managing relationships.

There is growing consensus that interpersonal communication is not a single thing, but rather, exists on a continuum from highly impersonal to highly interpersonal. The more personally we interact with another as a distinct individual (versus communicating in a general social role), the more interpersonal the communication is. Using this criterion, we would say that a deep conversation with a friend is more interpersonal than a casual exchange with a sales clerk.

Since the late 1960s, interest in interpersonal communication has mushroomed, making it one of the most vibrant branches of the communication field. Scholars focus on how communication creates and sustain relationships, how partners communicate to deal with the normal and extraordinary challenges of maintaining intimacy over time, and how media shape our expectations of and communication in relationships. Of particular concern to scholars of interpersonal communication are the ways romantic partners and close friends use communication to create and sustain intimacy. Research indicates that communication is the lifeblood of close relationships, since it is how friends and couples develop intimacy and how they continuously refashion relationships to meet their changing needs and preferences. Intimates who learn how to understand and talk with each other have the greatest chance of enduring over time.

Interpersonal communication researchers also study how communication is influenced by gender, ethnicity, and sexual orientation. Interpersonal communication is one of the fastest growing areas in the field.

The theory of interpersonal knowledge is the brain child of Charles Berger (1991) and his colleagues. It deals primarily with the ways in which individuals know themselves and others in interaction. The theory has two major concerns: self-awareness and knowledge of others. Self-awareness varies from person to person and from situation to situation. The enduring trait of being self-aware is self-consciousness, and this characteristic is dominated by a tendency to self-monitor, or "watch you."

Uncertainty Reduction Theory is a useful theory in interpersonal communication. The goal of this theory is to explain how communication reduces uncertainties. Berger (1979) thought that people want to predict and explain what goes on in their initial interactions with strangers. Prediction is the ability to define in advance what we or our relational partner will do or say.

Gender Theory is also useful in communication. The differences that being male or female create in communication are potential barriers to communication effectiveness. In terms of gender, it is useful sometimes to know the cultural norms, such as the idea that language and communication in the classroom reflect a culture's gender lenses and those norms can be reversed or made equitable.

Interpersonal communication occurs when two or more persons are involved in an interaction that allows all participants to send overt verbal messages. Conversations, interviews, committee meetings and group discussions are examples of interpersonal communication situations.

The basic unit of interpersonal communication is the dyad, which is defined as communicative interaction between two people.
The goals of dyadic communication are:

1. To exchange affection giving and receiving love.
2. To be sociable—sometimes we simply want to appear cordial, congenial, friendly. We interact with one another as if to say, "You're here; I'm here; the situation is casual and non threatening, so let's just relax and chat with one another."
3. To complete a task. While such associations may be friendly, they are not always so. Yet they usually continue because people subordinate personal feelings to the task of goal completion.
4. To share ideas and information. We like to discover what others think and know, and we like even better to tell them what we know.
5. To teach and learn. These dyads develop because of special skills of one person and special needs of another.
6. To persuade. An example is the door-to-door vendor. Some dyads become coercive as the persuader goes beyond the bounds of cooperative behavior and uses threats or force to gain agreement.
7. To heal—therapeutic reasons.
8. To resolve conflict. A husband and wife try to make up after a bitter argument.

## SELF DISCLOSURE

Interpersonal communication research is extensive on the topic of self disclosure and its effects on relationships. The conventional wisdom, born out of early studies, contends that relationships cannot fully develop into intimacy without both partners sharing information about them. Without self disclosure, we form superficial relationships.

The degree of understanding in a relationship depends in part on the openness of the relationship. Openness consists of both sensitivity and disclosure.

Sensitivity is a person's ability and willingness to perceive the other person accurately. It involves attention to and awareness of the cues presented by the other person. Sensitive communicators listen well and relate what they see and hear to the particular situation.

The other element of openness, self disclosure, involves revealing things about the self to another person. Interpersonal understanding can occur only when communicators disclose not only factual information, but also here-and-now feelings.

By disclosing information about the self, especially the things held dear (values, attitudes and beliefs), one is seeing how other people react to the self concept. Disclosing very intimate things about the self and having those things reinforced can have a powerful influence on the self-concept.

## SELF WITHHOLDING

Self disclosure also carries with it a risk. It is the risk that instead of the self-concept being reinforced, it will be shot down. The more one reveals about the self, the more hurt there can be if one's qualities are not accepted positively. "We always hurt the one[s] we love."

Another reason for avoiding self disclosure is the fear of revealing the self to the self. Everyone can be guilty of simply not admitting the truth to the self about the self.

### When Do We Self Disclose?

Research has taught that people tend to disclose things about themselves at different points in a relationship, as that relationship develops. Moreover, people tend to disclose negative things about themselves if at all much later, for the reason of impression management. Everyone wants to be liked and respected and to make a positive impression when first meeting people. Thus, people stress their positive qualities. As a relationship develops, people may feel less threatened by disclosing negative information.

### Reasons for Self Disclosure

1. Relationship maintenance
2. Relationship enhancement

3. Reciprocity—give, receive
4. Impression formation
5. Self clarification

## BECOMING AWARE OF SELF DISCLOSURE

Responsible communicators are aware of their own and other people's self disclosure.

1. Monitor the intentions for self disclosing information.
2. Amount of self disclosure: Monopolizing a conversation can leave the impression of being self centered or insensitive to the rules of relationship that demand appropriate self disclosure.
3. Being aware of the value of self disclosure helps one monitor the impressions presented to others. People who continually say negative things about themselves can leave the impression that they possess a low self-concept and are incompetent.
4. The depth of self disclosure is closely related to how far advanced a relationship is.
5. The accuracy of self disclosure: Being sincere and truthful is necessary for mutual trust in a relationship.

## ASSERTIVE COMMUNICATION

Assertion does not involve putting one's needs above those of others. Assertion is a matter of clearly and nonjudgmentally stating what one feels, need or want. Assertiveness is useful in all aspects of our lives, but it is essential in work situations. This is particularly true where you have an unequal status relationship.

To be assertive means that regardless of the difference in status levels between you and others, you are aware of the basic rights that parallel your responsibilities and are willing and able to assert these rights. You will be listened to and probably respected if you assert yourself.

### Rights to Be Assertive

1. You have the right to judge your own behavior, thoughts, and emotions and to take the responsibility for them and their consequences.
2. You have the right to stay out of other people's affairs.
3. You have a right to offer no excuses to justify your behavior.

4. You have the right to change your mind.
5. You have the right to say "I don't know".

## Acceptance of Self

*Assertive Behaviors*

1. Persistence
2. Compromise
3. Feedback
4. Appropriate self disclosure
5. Fogging (You cope with criticism and respond to it without becoming emotionally involved or anxious.)

The ability to communicate feelings, attitudes, and beliefs honestly and directly is a communication skill associated with a positive self-concept. Non assertiveness, conversely, is associated with a negative self-concept and indicates an inability to stand up for one's own rights or indicates that one stands up for oneself in a dysfunctional way. Nonassertive people do not acknowledge self. They do not accept the notion of personal rights and are inhibited in their expression of feelings, attitudes, and beliefs. Nonassertive people rarely achieve their goals and may often be hurt by other people. Perhaps nonassertive people feel their goal in life is to appease others or to serve others.

Assertiveness is different from aggressiveness. Aggressiveness involves standing up for one's rights at the expense of others. Aggressive people care little about anyone's needs, other than their own. They strive to win, regardless of the cost to others. People who interact with aggressive persons often feel a great deal of frustration. Aggressive people, like nonassertive people, probably suffer from a negative self-concept. They may feel insecure or unworthy of acceptance and believe they must compete to be accepted by others.

People who are assertive are concerned with their own needs and rights, as well as the needs and rights of others. Assertive people trust themselves and their responses. They are able to create a supportive communication climate marked by openness and honesty. The acceptance of personal rights and the lack of inhibition surrounding self-expression on the part of the assertive communicator encourage effective communication.

## WAYS TO IMPROVE RELATIONSHIPS
## THROUGH COMMUNICATION

Communicating with relational partners can be exciting, complex and sometimes confusing. Researchers in communication recommend an understanding of theories of symbolic interaction, uncertainty reduction, social penetration, social exchange and relational dialectics.

With symbolic interaction theory developed by Mead and analyzed by Larossa and Reitzes (1993) has assumptions that apply to interpersonal communication.

1. Humans act toward others on the basis of the meanings others have for them.
2. Meaning is created in interaction between people.
3. Meaning's are modified through an interpretive process
4. Individuals develop self concepts through interaction with others.
5. People and groups are influenced by cultural and social interaction.

With uncertainty reduction theory by Berger and Celabrese (1975) the message is that communication reduces uncertainties and is based on the following assumptions:

1. People experience uncertainty in interpersonal settings.
2. Uncertainty is an aversive state generating cognitive stress
3. Interpersonal communication is a developmental process that occurs through stages.
4. Interpersonal communication is the primary means of uncertainty reduction.

Social penetration theory articulated by Altman and Taylor (1973) refers to the movement from superficial communication to more intimate communication during the process of relationship development. The assumptions are:

1. Relationships progress from nonintimate to intimate
2. Relational development is generally systematic and predictable
3. Relational development includes depenetration and dissolution
4. Self disclosure is the core of relationship development

Social exchange theory developed by Thibaut and Kelly (1959) is on the notion that people think about their relationship in economic terms, adding up the costs involved and comparing those costs to the available rewards. Assumptions flow from the notion that people view like as a marketplace:

1. Humans seek rewards and avoid punishment
2. Humans are rational beings
3. Relationships are interdependent
4. Relational life is a process

Relational dialectics developed by Baxter and Montgomery (1996) theorize that what characterizes relational life is ongoing tensions between contradictory desires. Assumptions are:

1. Relationships are not linear.
2. Relational life is characterized by change.
3. Contradiction is the fundamental fact of relational life.
4. Communication is central to organizing and negotiating relational contradictions.

## Practical Tips for Improving Relationships

1. Active listening
2. Showing more respect by:
   a. Being a good listener
   b. Not interrupting
   c. Being honest
3. Be more empathic; try to feel what the other is experiencing.
4. Be patient.
5. Learn to deal with anger; instead of burying it, deal with it at an appropriate time.
6. Give positive feedback.
7. Be aware of one's own signals; listen to and try to understand one's self:
   a. Taking time alone for relaxation, prayer or meditation, etc.
   b. Being more aware of one's body, and others' non verbal language.
8. Be aware of timing.
9. Let go of having to win and having to be right all the time.
10. Acknowledge the feelings of others.
11. Be willing to compromise.
12. Be willing to accept total (100%) responsibility for the relationship when that is necessary.
13. When someone is complaining and critical, use active listening and I-messages, rather than becoming defensive.
14. Treat others as you want to be treated; encourage openness.
15. Be aware of others' needs, and let them know that you are by your feedback.
16. Try to have a positive attitude; use problem-solving methods, rather than criticism: focusing on the "good" helps build the other's self- image.
17. Build trust by practicing these things.
18. Remember, one positive "I-message" erases about one thousand "You-messages".

Relationships play a central role in determining the type of communication that is most effective and appropriate. In turn, competent interpersonal communication permits more meaningful relationships to develop. Each of you is involved in a number of relationships of different levels of importance. If you become aware that someone likes you, then your evaluation of her or him is apt to move toward liking.

## DEVELOPING AND MAINTAINING RELATIONSHIPS

Interpersonal communication, like all behavior, is goal-oriented, aimed at satisfying important needs and motivations.

### Elements in Personal Relationships

*Roles and Role Performance*

Individuals embark on relationships with their self concepts, personal experiences, preferred styles of communication and thinking, individual goals and the like. All these characteristics profoundly influence how they will communicate in any given conversation or relationship.

A role refers to a set of behaviors expected of people who occupy specific positions in a social relationship. The term role refers to expectations, as in, "What is the role of parent?" What a person does in a social position is called role performance. Understanding the effects of role in communication involves recognizing both role expectations and role performances. Each person, each group, and each society expects certain behaviors from people (parents, for example); and each reacts strongly to people who violate the expectations.

*Norms*

Norms refer to a standard of expected behavior for the violation of which people must pay a social penalty. Norms greatly influence communication. Choosing to ignore social norms leads to penalties, which vary according to the strength of the norm, how much it was violated, and how it applies to a particular situation. Nudity is a good example. Nudity can get people arrested in some places; but it will bring paying patrons to a movie, and it has brought a fortune to the creator of "Playboy".

Many cultural rules and norms are observed unconsciously and are not thought about until they are ignored or broken. That is, you take the rules and norms of your culture for granted; you typically follow them; and you expect your communication partners to follow them.

## STAGES OF RELATIONSHIP

When you begin to initiate a relationship, you are probably uncertain about your potential partner.

1. Initiation. Get more data to
   a. make an invitation
   b. direct us whether or not to accept an invitation if offered by the other
   c. casual status. Use non threatening rejectors if necessary
2. Sparring. Information seeking, testing roles, one against the others. Phatic communication. Sniff each other out. Check on first decision. Both relational partners want to reduce uncertainty.
3. Possibilities. Negotiate opportunities in the relationship. Rehearse internally. Identification of the other person. Note emotional intensity. Growth through recreational companionship. Bonding.
4. Intensification. Partners made an investment in each other and can afford to intensify their relationship
5. Medium of exchange
6. Stabilization stage. Perceptions of rewards and costs become more stable, comfortable providing a measure of predictability in the relationship.
7. Note situational changes.

## GENERAL ANALYSIS OF A RELATIONSHIP

1. Nature of the situation. Control, maintenance
2. Nature of the participants. Who talks to whom? Goal of the general situation. Long-term goals, short-term goals.
3. Roles. Roles deployed to each other. Role changes. Effect of role change.
4. Analysis of Norms. Methods for rule making; methods for rule changing.
5. Analysis of economics. Nature of exchange. Time, goods, services. Sentiments. Negotiation.
6. Analysis of prognosis. Has this relationship existed before this encounter? Goal, situation, role, stake, economics of exchange, awareness of exchange, reciprocity, bonding evidenced by claiming fouls, hurt and failure to meet obligations, maintenance.
7. Attitude similarity. Similar attitudes also produce increased liking. People are attracted to those who share their attitudes.

## IMPROVING RELATIONSHIPS

### Building Trust

Intimate relationships rarely develop or, more importantly, last without trust. The word trust refers to having a confident belief in someone.

## Sources of Trust

*Propensity to Trust*

For trust to develop, communicators must perceive each other as trustworthy. For some, that is easy. Some people believe that everyone is basically good: trust everyone; basically bad: harm others if given the opportunity.

## The Situation

Most people develop trust on the basis of specific experiences. Trust develops when you have communicated with a person or a group of people and found that your confidence in the positive outcomes of their behavior was justified.

## Acceptance

Acceptance is the ability to relate to another person without judging or trying to control that person.

## Empathy

Empathy means to experience the feelings of another person. Empathy contributes to trust because it helps communicate the attitude of acceptance.

## Honesty

Honesty in interpersonal relationships is the foundation of trust.

## INTERPERSONAL RELATIONSHIPS

### Emotional Intelligence

Emotional intelligence is the ability to understand and get along with others. It includes self awareness, managing emotions, motivating the self, recognizing emotion in others, and handling relationships.

### Self-Awareness

Self-awareness requires the ability to get a long distance from the emotion so that you can look at it without being overwhelmed by it or reacting to it too quickly. Distancing yourself from an emotion should not be a denial of it. Rather, it is a way to articulate to yourself what you are feeling so that you can act on it appropriately.

## Managing Emotions

Managing emotions means to express them in a manner appropriate to the circumstances. Anxiety and depression. Managing our emotions is not to say that we never feel angry, worried or depressed. These emotions are all part of being human. And if we don't find a way to express them, they could result in depression or antisocial acts. For emotional intelligence, it is important that we control them, rather than letting them control us.

## Motivating Yourself

Goal setting. Self-motivation involves resisting impulses and positive thinking and optimism. Rather than dwell on the failure, look at ways for improvement.

## Recognizing Emotions in Others

Empathy, the ability to recognize and share someone else's feelings, is essential in human relationships. Hearing what people are really saying. Reading body language such as gestures, facial expression, and tone of voice. People who are popular, outgoing, and sensitive, are all able to use empathy. Empathy has a strong moral dimension. Being able to recognize and share someone's distress means that you will not want to hurt him or her. Sharing empathy with others also means that you are able to reach out and help them.

## THE STAGES OF A RELATIONSHIP

1. Initiating (first impressions). We often decide the other person is not interesting enough or does not seem to want to pursue a relationship with us.
2. Experimenting. Experimenting is making a conscious effort to seek out common interests and experiences—expressing ideas, attitudes and values and seeing how the other person reacts. Many relationships stay at this particular stage. The participants enjoy the level of the relationship, but show no desire to pursue it.
3. Intensifying. Swapping cassettes and CDs and spending free time together exemplifies intensification of the relationship. In the intensification stage, people enjoy each other's company, open up to each other. They share frustrations, imperfections, and prejudices. They develop shorthand ways of speaking and jokes that no one else understands. In this stage, the relationship develops shared assumptions and expectations. Trust becomes important as do expressions of commitment. Self disclosure makes the relation-

ship strong but also makes the participants more vulnerable to each other.

4. Integrating. Individual personalities begin to merge. This stage is reached only when people develop deep and important relationships. Those who reach this stage are usually best friends, couples, or parents and children.
5. Bonding. Formal commitment.

Advancing from Stage One to Stage Five depends on both participants. If one wants to move to the next stage, it will not be possible unless the other agrees. Do not progress too quickly beyond Stages One or Two. Sensitivity to the feedback of others.

## COMING APART

1. Differentiating. No more interdependence. Focus on differences. Conversation is about differences, rather than similarities. If differences are not too great, can be worked out. Conflict.
2. Circumscribing. Superficial conversation. Discussion of safe topics.
3. Stagnating. Inactivity. Relationship has no chance to grow. When partners communicate, they talk like strangers.
4. Avoiding. Physical separation. Face-to-face interaction. Unfriendliness, hostility and antagonism. One takes the couch.
5. Termination. Differences are emphasized and communication is difficult and awkward.

## ESSENTIAL ELEMENTS OF GOOD RELATIONSHIPS

1. Commitment. Commitment is a relation of binding and being bound, giving and being claimed.
2. Expectations.
3. Dialogue. Ongoing conversations about relationship.
4. Listening.

## HANDLING RELATIONSHIPS

Expectations play a central role in forming the proper interpersonal messages in relationships. When people enter into relationships, they form ideas as to what they think will or should happen. Expectations have a way of influencing how people act and feel toward others. You may form expectations not only about the individual with whom you have a relationship, but also about the relationship itself.

Most popular are largely positive and energetic people. Being with them makes us positive, too. They are also the people who organize others, negotiate solutions when there is a problem to be solved, and generally connect with others emotionally; they have a sense of balance.

## RECOGNIZING OWN NEEDS AND KNOWING HOW TO FULFILL THEM.

### Attraction to Others

Often we are attracted to others because of the way they look. We like someone's appearance and want to get to know the person better. In some cases, physical attraction may be sexual attraction. In most cases, however, attraction goes beyond physical appearance. Sometimes we are attracted to people because of the way they dress. They choose a style of clothing that is our own style or is a style we would like to imitate. They have a certain look that we like very much. Physical attraction, then, can be a reason for getting to know someone. It is seldom the only basis for a long-term relationship.

### Perceived Gain

Sometimes we are attracted to people because we think we have something to gain from associating with them. Other people like to make friends with those who have status or power, hoping that this association will confer status and power on them, as well.

### Similarities

Often we are attracted to people because we like what they say. We are attracted when we discover that they share our attitudes and beliefs or they seem knowledgeable about topics we find interesting and significant.

### Beliefs—Our Convictions

### Attitudes—Our Deeply Held Beliefs

### Differences

Although two people who have very different beliefs are unlikely to form a strong and lasting relationship, people with different personality characteristics might well be attracted to each other. For example, a person who doesn't like making decisions might be attracted to a strong decision maker. Because these qualities complement each other, they might help strengthen the relationship.

## Proximity

Proximity is defined as close contact that occurs when people share an experience such as work, play, or school. Through this contact, people meet their friends and often find their mates.

## EXPRESSING YOUR FEELINGS VERBALLY

Feeling the warmth, support, acceptance, and caring of close friendships is one of the most exciting aspects of being alive. Feelings are especially wonderful when they are shared with other people.

One of the most rewarding aspects of relationships is sharing personal feelings. The more you share your feelings with other people, the happier and more meaningful your life will be. To experience emotions and express them to another person is not only a major source of joy, it is also necessary for your psychological well-being.

It is natural to have feelings. Feeling and expressing caring for another person, feeling and expressing love for another person, even feeling and expressing anger toward another person are all potentially highly rewarding and beautiful experiences.

## WHEN FEELINGS ARE NOT EXPRESSED

We all have feelings about the people with whom we interact and share experiences, but many times we do not communicate these feelings effectively. Several difficulties arise when feelings are not recognized, accepted, and expressed constructively.

1. Suppressing and denying feelings can create relationship problems.
   a. increased conflict
   b. deterioration in the relationship
   c. suppressed anger
   d. withdrawal
2. Suppressing and denying feelings interferes with the constructive diagnosis and resolution of relationship problems. Conscious, discussable, and controllable.

3. Denying feelings can result in selective perceptions.

4. Suppressing feelings can bias judgment. If you are aware of your feelings and manage them constructively—unbiased and objective in judgment. Implying a demand while expressing feelings can create a power struggle. Many times, feelings are expressed in ways that demand change in the receiver's behavior.

## EXPRESSING YOUR FEELINGS VERBALLY

### Verbal—Non Verbal

To communicate clearly, your verbal and nonverbal expression of feelings must agree. Communicating your feelings depends on your being aware of your feelings, accepting them, and being skillful in expressing them constructively. Describing your feelings to another person often helps you become more aware of what it is you actually do feel. Explaining them to another person often clarifies our feelings to ourselves, as well as to the other person. Describing your feelings will improve your relationship. When discussing your relationship with another person, describing your feelings conveys maximum information about what you feel in a more constructive way than giving commands, asking questions, making accusations or offering judgments.

## SUGGESTED ACTIVITIES

### Increasing Intimacy

*Objective*

To have students suggest ideas for increasing closeness in relationships.

*Procedure*

I need you in groups of from four to six students each. Within the group, I want you, as a group, to think of as many ideas for increasing closeness as you can. Have one group member (the recorder) write down your ideas. After you have generated a list of items, stop and rank order them, with number one as the most important.

*Discussion*

I am going to ask groups to report now. Just your top one or two items only, please. (Place the top item[s] on the chalk board. By a show-of-hands, vote on them, and rank order the items as a class.)

## Some Suggestions For Increasing Intimacy

Spend time planning the future.
  Five years from now
  Ten years from right now
Share goals, dreams, and plans.
Reminisce about the past.
  The thing I liked best about our past was . . .
  The thing I thought was the most fun when we were dating was . . .
Take an extended vacation together.
Plan an intimate night out together.
Talk about each other to better understand yourselves—as a joint venture.
  As a kid I . . .
  In my family, we would . . .
  One of the traditions in my family that I loved was . . .
Share fantasies, nightmares, and images.
  The wildest fantasy I have ever had was . . .
  The scariest nightmare I have ever had was . . .
  The image that recurs most often for me is . . .
Do something brand new and exciting together.
Share silliness.
Speak in special voices.
Make up special characters together.
Develop some special facial expressions which communicate special meanings just for the two of you.
  Be spontaneous.
    When I get crazy, I like to . . .
  Engage in shared deviant experiences.
    Something that we could do that would be absolutely "off the wall"
would be to . . .

### Discussion

Could these items also be used to revitalize relationships that are not intimate?
What is it that makes it necessary to increase intimacy, or to revitalize relationships? Should we just want to do it?
What are likely barriers or constraints to increasing intimacy?

*Chapter Ten*

# Culture and Communication

Devito (2007) defines culture as relatively specialized lifestyles of a group of people. It includes values, beliefs, artifacts, behavior, general ways of communication, language, modes of thinking, art, laws, morals, religion.

Culture involves enculturation and acculturation. Enculturation is the process by which we learn the culture in which we are born. Acculturation is the process by which we learn the rules and norms of a culture different from native culture. Acculturation modifies both cultures.

In intercultural communication both parties may have slight or great differences in beliefs, values, or ways of behaving. Messages originate from a specific unique cultural context. Cultural context acts as filters through which we receive messages.

## HOW CULTURES DIFFER

Devito (2007) tells us that cultures differ in the following ways:

1. Power distances or the extent to which power is concentrated in a few citizens or distributed throughout the citizenry. Power distance is demonstrated in attitudes toward friendship, dating, authority, and symbols of power.
2. Masculine and feminine cultures emphasize success and socialize people to be assertive and competitive. In masculine cultures men are encouraged to be strong and independent; women, modest and tender. In feminine societies, both men and women are socialized toward concern for quality of life.
3. Individual and collective cultures promote individual or collective values.

4. High or low context cultures deals with the extent to which information is made explicit in the verbal message or assumed into the context or relationship.

Human differences result in the potential for misunderstanding and miscommunication. Effective communicators adapt their messages to others. Culture and communication are clearly linked because of the powerful role culture plays in influencing our values. Cultural values reflect how individuals regard masculine/feminine, the importance of tolerating uncertainty or preferring certainty, the preference for centralized or decentralized power structures, and the valuing of individual or collective accomplishment.

Intercultural communication refers to the process of understanding and sharing meaning with individuals from various cultures. Some scholars make fine distinctions among interracial, interethnic, cross cultural, contra-cultural, and trans-cultural acts.

Not long ago, intercultural communication involved only missionaries, jet setting business executives, foreign correspondents, diplomatic personnel, and some national political figures. These individuals were few in number. Most people in the United States interacted with other people like themselves. Now, however, developments in technology and shifts in demographics have created a society where intercultural communication is nearly inevitable for everyone.

Today, communication satellites, digital switches, and fax machines instantly connect all parts of the world. Traveling to other countries once took days; now it is possible to make the same trip in a matter of hours. Population shifts and new developments in technology have created one world community. We have truly become the global village. No nation, group or culture is isolated. Contact with people who are different from us is something for which each person must be prepared.

Communication is closely linked to culture because communication creates, expresses, sustains, and alters cultural life. Your culture directly shapes how you communicate, teaching you whether it is polite to interrupt, how much eye contact is appropriate, whether individuality is desirable, and whether argument and conflict are healthy.

The intimate relationship between communication and culture has inspired a number of theories. Three have earned high regard. The broadest of the three is Standpoint Theory, which traces the ways in which the locations of distinct social groups within a society shape members' experiences, knowledge, and ways of interacting. Speech Communication Theory offers a more specific analysis of the same issue with its focus on how interaction with particular social groups shapes styles of communication that differ for women, men, and members of different ethnicities. Finally, we consider Organizational Culture Theory, which illuminates the role of communication in creating and sustaining distinct cultures in organizational life.

In one excellent example of a study in the area of personal relationships among co-workers, communication scholar Ted Zorn (1998) reports on "bosses and buddies"—people involved in friendships in which one friend is the boss of the other. Zorn discovered a number of ways people cope with the often contradictory rules for communication between friends and between superiors and subordinates. He also points out both potential values and hazards of friendships in which one person has formal power over another.

Personal relations on the job also require that women and men learn to understand each other's language. In a number of ways, women and men communicate differently, and they frequently misunderstand one another. For example, women tend to make more listening noises, such as um, uh-huh, and go on, than men do. If men don't make such noises when listening to women colleagues, the women may think the men aren't paying attention. Conversely, men are likely to misinterpret the listening noises women make as signals of agreement, rather than as indications of interest. Such misunderstandings can strain professional relations and performance. Some scholars or communication organizations study and conduct workshops on effective communication between the sexes.

Intercultural communication refers to communication between people from different cultures, including distinct cultures within a single country. Although intercultural communication is not a new area of study, it is one whose importance has grown in recent years. Demographic shifts in the last decade have enlarged the diversity that has always marked life in the United States. Increasing numbers of Asians, Indians, Latinas and Latinos, and people of other nations are immigrating to the United States and making their homes here. With them, they bring cultural values and styles of communicating that differ from those of citizens whose heritage is European American. Understanding different modes of verbal and nonverbal communication can help us learn how to live, socialize and work effectively with an ever-increasing range of people.

A particularly important recent trend in the area of intercultural communication is research on different communication cultures within a single society. Cultural differences are easy to perceive in communication between a Nepali and a Canadian. Less obvious are cultural differences in communication between people who speak the same language. Within the United States, there are distinct communication cultures that are based on race, gender, affectional preference, and ethnicity.

## DEFINING CULTURAL IDENTITY

Cultural identity is a broad way of looking at cultural groups at various levels, including assumptions, underlying values, social relations, customs and overall outlook on life that differ significantly among groups.

Cultural identity is concerned with characteristics that people use or distinguish their ways of thinking and behaving from those of others; e.g., world's great religions—Islam, Buddhism, and Christianity—are often used as cultural distinctions with regard to values, beliefs, and the like.

When people proclaim fidelity to specific customs, traditions, languages, and religions, they can and do define their identity as a result of such compositions and shapes.

This way of marking boundaries between ourselves and others explains a great deal about why people think and act as they do. It explains why one says with such firmness and commitment: "I am Russian," "African," or "Middle Eastern."

Another way of looking at cultural identity is to say it helps people to comprehend the formation of that pronoun "we" and to reckon with patterns of inclusion and exclusion that it cannot help creating.

Cultural identity helps people reckon with who belongs to their group and who does not belong. Solidarity groups and cultural entities

Although I am talking about cultural identities, I am not explaining how cultural identities evolve as it will require complex phenomena.

What is important, however, is that once humans define themselves as belonging to one cultural group as opposed to another, they attach great importance to such belonging.

Finally, cultural identity serves as an interpretive device. We see ourselves along such dimensions as race, ethnicity, kinship, soil, region, gender, and religion. The categories, in turn, help us know who we are, what we want, and where we wish to go. Interpretation affects our communication and the stories we tell.

## FORMATION OF CULTURAL IDENTITY

The three stages in the formation of identity are the unexamined cultural identity, cultural identity search and cultural identity achievement.

### Unexamined Cultural Identity

Unexamined cultural identity includes things we take for granted in our level of consciousness. Young children, for example, are unaware of the characteristics that distinguish one culture from another. As children grow older, they become mindful of categories and who belongs to a particular culture. Parents, the media, social memberships, and other sources play a role in helping individuals understand what is meant by cultural identity.

## Cultural Identity Search

To identify cultural search sometimes involve a questioning mode about one's culture. By the asking questions one might understand cultural memberships and implications of such memberships. The effect of activities and media such as chatting with family and friends, attending festivals, going to museums, watching films and television and so on also helps in identity search. The individual comes to know that he or she belongs to cultural group A as opposed to cultural group B.

As individuals become more aware of their culture, they develop an emotional attachment to their own cultural group with emotional intensity.

Cultural identity achievement involves an internalization of individuals' attachment to their group. People are clear and confident about personal meanings of their culture and can deal with such matters as stereotypes and discrimination without internalizing others negative perceptions and. using qualities of their culture to guide their future actions.

## CHARACTERISTICS OF CULTURAL IDENTITY

### Gender in Culture

Women traditionally have a historical and cultural identity significantly different from that of men.

Until recently men have argued differences were based on biological differences. Women: emotional and nurturing. Men: rational, strong.

Gender is influenced by both social structure and cultural development.

All cultures differentiate between male and female behavior.

Social Constructions tell us that throughout our interaction with others, we receive constant messages that reinforce female's conformity to femininity and males to masculinity.

Therefore, gender is a social creation.

### Ethnicity

Ethnicity is concerned with real and presumed ancestry, a common history that is apart from others, interaction among members who share a consciousness of kind attachment to the past.

Two of the leading writers about intercultural communication are Larry Samovar and Richard Porter.D (1982). They reveal distinctive styles of communication for women, blacks, whites, Native Americans, Gays, individuals with disabilities, and other groups in our country. For example, women more than men tend to disclose personal information and to engage in emotionally expressive talk in their friendships. African Americans belong to a communication culture that encourages dramatic talk, rappin', verbal duels, and signifying (indirect comments) which have no equivalents in Caucasian speech communities. Recognizing and respecting different communication cultures increases effectiveness in a pluralistic society.

## SUGGESTED ACTIVITIES

Rank order the following 11 statements to indicate those statements you believe in most (1) to those statements you believe in least (11).

- It is the person who stands alone who excites our admiration.
- There should be equality for everyone, because we are all human beings.
- The purpose of our existence is not to attain happiness but to be worthy of it.
- The person who has achieved success has lived well, laughed often, and loved much.
- A well-raised child is one who doe not have to be told twice to do something.
- Let us eat, drink, and be merry, for tomorrow we may die.
- A rich life requires constant activity, the use of one's muscles, and openness to adventure.
- Friendship should only go so far in working (business) relationships.
- To lay down your life for a friend—this is the summit of a good life.
- We are all born to love; it is the principle of existence and its only true end.
- The past is dead; there are new worlds to conquer; the world belongs to the future.

### Examples of Arguments Reflecting Cultural Assumptions

Read the following three scenarios and choose the answer that best explains each situation.

1. A murder has been committed, and one man has been accused of the crime. You want to know whether he is guilty or innocent. You should:
   a. Observe the accused man. Guilty people usually give themselves away in how they talk or act.

   b. Look for physical evidence. You must find some footprint, fingerprint, or property that connects the accused man with the crime.
   c. Find witnesses. You should talk with all who know the accused man, were at the scene of the crime, etc.
   d. Put the accused person to a test and see how he behaves. This might be a psychological test or some physical test that will give you proof.
2. You are a very fortunate person. You are happy, healthy, and intelligent. You have a strong and loving family. Almost everything you set out to do turns out well. You think:
   a. I am just lucky. Some people are lucky, some people are not. I happen to be lucky.
   b. I must be careful; good and bad tend to balance, and one of these days things will begin to go badly for me.
   c. Life is what you make it. To be happy you have to "think happy," as happiness is all up to the individual's attitude and frame of mind.
   d. Somebody or some force is watching over me. Call it "God" or a guardian angel or some other supernatural power—I have such faith.
3. You are a farmer. There has been a long, dry spell throughout the growing season, and there is little hope for rain soon. Without rain, you and your family may starve during the next year. What is the best thing for you to do?
   a. Pray for rain. Only God (or the gods) can deliver you from this dry spell.
   b. Ask scientists or technical people for methods to create rain, perhaps by seeding the clouds with chemicals.
   c. Ask the elders and wise-men of the community; they have lived the longest, and they know best what to do.
   d. You are probably being punished; the dry spell is a curse. Discover the source of this curse, remove it, and the rains will come.

## IMPACT OF SOCIAL CHANGE AND TECHNOLOGY

On July 3, 1999 the Pew Research Center for the People and the Press published a report titled *Technology Triumphs, Morality Falters*. A survey of people across the United States was conducted to ascertain how life had changed for the better or worse throughout the twentieth century and in the decade of the 1990s.

Among the topics they asked people to evaluate were a number of social trends and technological advances that impact our lives in a positive or a negative manner. In the scales below make your assessments. For each item, check off whether you think it has changed things for the better, for the worse, or that no change has occurred.

- The invention of the computer
- Women in the workplace
- Invention of birth control pills
- Legalization of abortion
- Invention of television
- Invention of the radio
- The Civil Rights Movement
- Airline travel
- The automobile
- Greater acceptance of divorce
- The interstate highway system
- Rock and Roll
- The internet and e-mail
- Viagra
- Rap music
- Immigration and cultural diversity
- Growth in telemarketing
- Cellular phones
- Cable tv
- Fertility drugs

Reflect about the changes that have occurred by answering one or more of the following critical questions;

1. How have the changes in the last century produced better or worse conditions for our lives? From the Pew study, reflect on several that you can highlight as having the most positive effect and those that have had a negative impact.
2. How have these changes affected the way that we develop a self-concept and relate to other people?
3. What changes would you add to the list, which you think have produced a positive or negative change?

Dr. Terrance Doyle

## CULTURAL RESUME

This activity involves summary and analysis of culture. It requires students to prepare a resume of a culture.

**Table 10.1.  Table of Countries**

| | | | |
|---|---|---|---|
| Algeria | Finland | Mexico | Scotland |
| Argentina | France | Netherlands | Sierra Leone |
| Australia | Germany | New Zealand | Spain |
| Austria | Greece | Nigeria | Sri Lanka |
| Belgium | Hong Kong | Norway | Sweden |
| Bolivia | Hungary | Pakistan | Switzerland |
| Brazil | Indonesia | Peru | Syria |
| Bulgaria | India | Paraguay | Tahiti |
| Canada | Iran | Philippines | Taiwan |
| Chile | Ireland | Poland | Thailand |
| Czechoslovakia | Israel | Portugal | Turkey |
| Denmark | Italy | Puerto Rico | Wales |
| Egypt | Jordan | Romania | Yugoslavia |
| England | Kenya | Russia | Zaire |
| Ethiopia | Lebanon | Samoa | Zimbabwe |
| Fiji | Malaysia | Saudi Arabia | Other |

## Competencies

1. To encourage students to become familiar with a specific culture in the process of summarizing its unique customs, traditions, values, and lifestyles.
2. To help students develop sensitivity toward the people of different cultures thus enabling them to communicate better with people from that culture.

From the table of countries; choose one to study.

## Demonstrating Achieving the Outcome

Students will research the country and its culture. Students will obtain and investigate and present information, by checking various sources of supporting materials both primary and secondary. Other research techniques include interviewing people from the culture or observing cultural traditions and rituals, visiting schools and local libraries, human relations area files, and computer-aided research systems, or relating personal experience, or expert opinion.

## Qualities to be Looked for in Student Performance

Students will have skills to organize useful answers for the following items which should be covered in cultural resume.

A. Customs and courtesies
   Greetings
   Gestures
   Travel
   Visiting

Personal Appearance
Communicating
Eating
Group Meetings
Interpersonally
B. The people
General attitudes and values
Religion
Population
Holidays, religious and political
Language
C. Lifestyle
Family
Work
Dating, courtship, and marriage
Recreation
Social and economic levels
Food
D. The Nation
History and government
Transportation and communication systems
Educational system
Health, sanitation, and medical facilities
Land and climate
Scale map of the country (placement can vary)
Economy

## Qualities that Will Distinguish Exemplary Student Performance from Satisfactory Performance

- Communication Style and Competence
- Contextual nature of communication
- Appropriateness
- Effectiveness
- Display of respect
- Orientation to knowledge
- Having Empathy
- Similarities and differences between cultures
- Motivation
- Interaction management

Adapted by Alusine M. Kanu from *Intercultural Communication Encounters*, 2007. Donald W.Klopf and James C. Mccroskey, Pearson: New York.

## BUILDING INTERCULTURAL SKILLS

There are skills necessary to communicate effectively across cultures:

1. Understanding cultural identity and history. Much communication, including intercultural communication, occurs at an unconscious level. To improve intercultural communication requires awareness of messages we send and receive, both verbal and non verbal.
2. Becoming more aware of others' communication. Understanding other people's communication requires the important intercultural skill of empathy; that is to say, knowing where someone else is coming from or "walking in their shoes."
3. Expand your own intercultural communication repertoire. This involves experimenting with different ways of looking at the world and of communicating verbally and non verbally. Building this skill may require that one step outside the comfort zone and look at things in a different light. It may require that one question ideas and assumptions.
4. Become more flexible in your communication. This involves avoiding what has been called "hardening of the categories."
5. Be an advocate for others. To improve intercultural communication among groups, everybody's voice must be heard. Improving relations among groups of people based on ethnicity, race, sex, physical ability, or whatever difference is not just about improving individual communication skills. It is also about forming coalitions with others.

# Chapter Eleven

# Small Groups:
# Concepts and Characteristics

There is probably no absolute definition of the small group. Rather, what we can do is to develop operational definitions based upon where and how and under what circumstances individuals meet and interact with other individuals in such a way that a sense of group is created.

Ivan Steiner (1972), in *Collective Action*, examines the impulses which lead to collective action. He illustrates how collective action satisfies individual needs and at the same time, creates dilemmas about which patterns of collective behavior are the most satisfactory. He states that, "Collective behavior may be examined at any of the three levels: the group, the organization or the society," and goes on to discuss the importance of defining the group in preparation for the study of *collective behavior*.

*The Social Group Definitions,* by Charles Palazzolo (1981), takes the position that a simple definition is not enough because a group involves a system of relations in which individuals become meaningful participants in a kind of *association* which is lasting and which is committed to the achievement of a goal or a *set of goals.*

Patrick Penland and Sara Fine (1974), in their essay on group dynamics tell us that "a *group is a system within a system within a system.*" They explain that every group is responsible to some larger system which becomes the reality base for that group. Every group is a product of the social context out of which it is created.

Groups require *communication rules* which govern the various aspects of group interaction. She discusses the following aspects of rule-governed group interaction: (1) types of rules, (2) emergence of rules, (3) functions and outcome of rules, and (4) factors influencing rule compliance. One can identify

the rules operative in a group (who says what to whom, when, with what du-
ration, medium, decision procedure).

Gerald Philips and Eugene Erickson (1994) consider what happens when
the individual enters a group. They assume that each *individual* possesses *desires and motives* which determine the approach to the group and the initial
interactions within the group. On the other hand, they maintain that any group
establishes *norms* and *rituals* which control or influence the activities of new
members. Individuals achieve personal goals but are also conforming members of the group.

Ernest Bormann (1990)—Each small group forms its own *culture* based on
*shared experiences* and values. Group members come to have an emotional
attachment to the group, and each group comes to have a culture that influences individuals within the group.

## Ways We Can Identify a Group

1. Perceptions—Do members make an impression on others?
2. Motivations—Is the group membership rewarding?
3. Goals—Working together for a purpose.
4. Organization—Each person has some organized role to play, such as moderator, note taker, etc.
5. Interdependency—Each person is somewhat dependent on the others.
6. Interaction—The group is small enough to allow fact-to-face communication among members.

## A DEFINITION

A group is a collection of individuals who influence one another, derive some
satisfaction from maintaining membership in the group, interact for some
purpose, assume some specialized roles, are dependent on one another, and
communicate face-to-face.

Small Group Interaction—The process by which three or more members of
a group exchange verbal and nonverbal messages in an attempt to influence
one another.

Small group interaction is very complicated and involves a large number
of factors which act and interact simultaneously. In addition, these factors are
in a continual state of flux. Think of the difficulty of trying to describe and
analyze all the behaviors that occur at just one party. We have all been to parties that generate far more reactions than we would have thought.

# MILLS MODELS—MODELS FOR STUDYING AND ANALYZING SMALL GROUPS

1. The Quasi-Mechanical Model
2. The Organismic Model
3. The Conflict Model
4. The Equlibrium Model
5. The Structural-Functional Model—goal
6. The Cybernetic Growth Model

1. The Quasi-Mechanical Model assumes that a group is like a machine. All behavioral acts in a group are seen as functions which can be categorized. Each functional act (e.g., a question) calls for a reaction (e.g., an answer). All actions and reactions are quantifiable and may be added, subtracted, multiplied or divided in such a way as to mathematically represent the dynamics of the group. Group behavior is considered to follow universal and unchanging laws. This model also assumes that people are merely interchangeable parts in the system and that all problem-solving groups will exhibit many of the same behaviors. Mills criticizes the Quasi-Mechanical Model as not telling us much about group discussion.

2. The Organismic Model assumes that groups are like biolobical organisms; that is, they have a period of formation (birth), a life cycle, and eventually, a death. Different people in the group become differentiated in their behaviors (e.g., task leader, recorder, social leader) just as bodily systems carry on different functions (e.g., digestive, respiratory, muscular). The emphasis is upon the group's natural evolution and development. Thus, this model severely reduces the methods for studying groups which might otherwise be employed.

3. The Conflict Model assumes that the small group is a context for an endless series of conflicts. All members of groups have to face the conflict of being truly independent versus conforming to some extent to the group norms and expectations. Also, since there are many groups with which to affiliate, individuals feel conflict in deciding which to join. Within the group, differences of opinion are a continuous source of potential conflict. Conflicts arise between groups as well. Mills argues that this model is too limited in that it tends to overlook all the socially binding factors in favor of the socially divisive factors; it is too one-sided.

4. The Equilibrium Model assumes that groups and group members have a need to maintain some sort of balance or equilibrium. For example, conflicts between group members tend to be followed by attempts to smooth over hard feelings and return to a state of interpersonal harmony.

*Balance Theory*. Although the Equilibrium Model gives us insight on a relatively simple level of analysis, when one adds in all the elements to be considered, the model is too limited to be able to explain much. For example, if I have an attitude toward a friend (positive), and he says something I don't like (negative), I can resolve this situation by agreeing with him or disliking him. But what if I forgive his comment and disagree with him on that issue, while continuing to like him?

5. The Structural-Functional Model assumes that the group is a goal-seeking system which is constantly adapting to meet the new demands. It assumes that the goal attainment is the primary source of satisfaction to its members. It also assumes that some members will take on the role of keeping the group functioning. These so-called group maintenance functions will serve to keep interpersonal relations from breaking down so that the group would cease functioning. This model is one of the better ones available because it includes the role of learning which helps groups survive by adapting to the demands for new behaviors.

6. The Cybernetic Growth Model shifts the emphasis from group survival to group growth. This model assumes the existence of group agents which help the group adapt to new information (or feedback). Thus, growth and development are attained by the group's responding to feedback from its earlier performance. Three types of feedback—goal seeking, group restructuring, and self-awareness—are required to help the group grow and develop. Mills argues that this model is strong in that it helps us identify the important factors or variables which lead to growth on the part of the group, as well as on the part of individual members.

## Importance and Needs for Groups

Groups are important to individuals and to society. Human beings use communication to share resources in the solution of problems; and group communication thereby becomes not only an instrument for accomplishing tasks, but also a means of group maintenance and cohesion. Group communication can be viewed as a system of inputs, internal processes, and outputs.

The process of group interaction involves two kinds of group energy: task energy and socio emotional energy. Task energy is directed at problem solving, and socio emotional energy is directed at group maintenance and interpersonal relationships.

Group problem solving is a developmental process. In other words, a group will go through different stages in its evolution. The character of the communication will vary from one stage to the next. Stages, however, are not easy to see in a group, because the group simultaneously operates on a variety of levels, and each level must be analyzed separately. The overall pattern of the group development is tracked along its unique configuration of actions at each level.

Under the aegis of conflict resolution, there are three poor ways to handle conflict: denial, suppression, and power. Two recommended ways to resolve conflict in a small group are compromise and collaboration.

> Accept human differences and limitations. Don't expect anyone to be perfect. Remember, the other person has a right to be different. And don't be a reformer.
>
> —David Schwartz

Small groups constitute the basic fabric of social life in the first part of the twenty-first century. We do not exist as humans alone, but as members of families, work groups, clubs and circles of friends.

Most of us spend a major portion of each day involved as members of various small groups. The higher a person goes in any organizational hierarchy, the more time the person spends in meetings of small groups and the greater the need for the skills and abilities.

Communication in small groups is so much a part of our lives that most of us take it for granted, failing to perceive and understand what is happening in these groups and how to make them more effective. We need to understand how to communicate more effectively in groups, or we are doomed to unsatisfying and ineffectual discussions.

Giffin and Patton wrote in 1971,

> Since the individual today is experiencing a growing dependency on groups of all descriptions, it is important that people be familiar with the dynamics of group interaction. Once a person has acquired an understanding of the nature of groups, the bases of their development, and their interrelationships with individuals and other groups, he has the basis for prediction and control.

We need membership in small groups for many reasons. We need small groups to meet distinctly human needs.

## Schutz (1987)

We need groups because they are more effective problem solvers in the long run than are individuals. Group members can see the blind spots and biases in each other's thinking, eliminating many faulty solutions and leaving as a remainder an idea that is better than any one member alone can devise.

Motivation of effort is required for participation in work planning or problem solving. People work harder and better when they have helped decide what to do. No plan of action is good if the people who must carry it out don't like it and work half-heartedly.

## STANDARDS FOR AN IDEAL DISCUSSION GROUP

The quality of any discussion group can only be determined from its outputs, its effectiveness. The interdependence of all components of a system is demonstrated as we seek to define the characteristics of an ideal discussion group. Since discussion is the name of the communication process when a small group meets, the emphasis in the abstract descriptions of an ideal discussion group follows is on the throughput variables, rather than input or output.

### Decision Making in Small Groups

Whether we like to acknowledge it or not, the need to make decisions in concert with others is becoming more and more important all the time as our society becomes more complex and interdependent.

Many choices have to be made in concert by members of small groups—when to meet, where to meet, whether or not to accept a statement as truth, whether or not a defendant is guilty, what punishment to mete, what reward to give, which applicant shall receive the scholarship, or which of several proposed solutions to recommend. Some discussions are relatively trivial; others, highly important.

Decision making refers to the act of choosing between two or more possible alternatives. Problem solving usually requires making numerous decisions before the group is ready to choose among several possible solutions to the problem and implement one.

Deciding among alternatives by a group rather than an individual invariably takes more time. A group of persons must often discuss at great length before making a decision. Time can be expensive. Certain types of decisions can be made better by an individual than by a group if an individual is truly expert in the matter and the group members are not.

Group decisions tend to be higher in quality than those made by individuals. Group decisions are more conservative than those of individuals. Groups make riskier decisions than individuals (polarization tendency). Group members tend to make either riskier or safer decisions than they did before the discussion.

**Table 11.1.   The Systems Perspective**

| Relevant Background Factors | Internal Influences | | Consequences |
|---|---|---|---|
| Personality | Physical Environment | Communication | Solutions |
| Sex | Group Size and structure | Language Behavior | Interpersonal relations |
| Age   ←→ | Type of Group | Self-disclosure   ←→ | Improved information flow |
| Health | Status and Power | Interaction roles | Risk taking |
| Attitudes | Leadership | Decision style | Interpersonal growth |
| Values | Group norms | Conflict | Organizational Change |

The Assembly Effect says that the decision is qualitatively and effectively superior to what could have been achieved by even the most expert member of the group or by adding or averaging the wisdom of the members because there is a sharing of responsibility.

Relevant background factors refers to attributes within the individual participants which exist prior to the group's formation and which will endure in some modified form after the group no longer exists. These background factors, such as personality, attitudes, and values, influence the group's functioning and vice versa. As a result of the group members' similarities in age, sex, attitudes, and values, we would expect a great deal less conflict in this group than we might expect if we added a few members who differed on these factors.

A second set of variables in the model is referred to as internal influences. These influences include (among others) the type of group, the style of leadership used, the language behavior, interaction roles, and decision style employed by the group. Each of these factors may be varied to change the nature and functioning of the group.

The third set of variables is the consequences of group interaction. Consequences will obviously vary with the background of the participants, as well as the nature of the internal influences. Consequences may include solutions to problems, interpersonal relations among group members, the amount and quality of information sharing, the level of risk taking, the amount of interpersonal growth of participants and possibly the amount of change in any larger organization of which the group may be a part.

A small group can best be understood as a system of interdependent components and forces. General Systems Theory is built on an analysis of living things which attempt to remain in dynamic balance with an environment by constant adjustments throughout the entire organism. Any system is active, living, dynamic—constantly changing. No system is ever static: a change in any part of an organism or its immediate environment reverberates throughout the entire system.

One benefit of thinking of the small group as a system is that this emphasizes the notion of multiple causation, which is to say that whatever happens is not the result of a single simple cause, but the result of complex interrelationships among many forces. Another benefit of the systems perspective is that it leads to looking for multiple outcomes of any change in the group. With a systems perspective, we are more likely to consider all of the characteristics of a group when trying to understand and improve its functioning, rather than looking at only one or two of them, thus possibly missing what is most important.

The variables (characteristics or dimensions) of a small group (or of any system) can be classified into three broad categories: input variables, throughput variables, and output variables.

Input variables are the components from which a small group is formed and which it uses to do work: members of the group, the reason for forming the group (for instance, the charge to a committee or the individual needs which members cannot meet acting alone), resources, such as information and tools and environmental conditions, and forces which influence or become part of the group's functioning.

Throughput variables include the structure of relationships among members and their roles, rules (norms) which emerge, procedures followed, communication among members, and all other things which are part of the processes of a group functioning to achieve some goals.

Output variables are the result of the group's throughput processes, especially tangible work accomplished (such as items built, policies developed, judgments made, and recommendations given to some larger organization), changes in the members themselves, effects of the group on its environment, and changes in the group's procedures themselves.

## DEVELOPMENT OF A GROUP

A number of writers have been interested in the social influence process as it is manifested in different stages or phases of group development. Group development seems to be partly the result of individual psychological needs and partly the result of the social influences manifested in the group.

One viewpoint is that phases occur in each meeting and continue to occur throughout the group's life history.

Phase 1 seems to be a period in which group members simply try to break the ice and begin to find out enough about one another to have some common basis for functioning. It is variously referred to as a period of *orientation, inclusion,* or group formation. In this phase, people ask questions about one another, tell where they are from, what they like and dislike, and generally make small talk.

Phase 1 seems to be characterized by the establishment of some *minimal social relationship* before group members feel comfortable getting down to work. However, some executives who have experienced many years of decision-making meetings may begin work with little or no social orientation and only the barest minimum of group orientation. However, with these exceptions, the vast majority of us feel better having some period to build relationships prior to launching into the group's work.

Phase 2 is frequently characterized by *conflict of some kind or other.* After the orientation phase passes, the pressure to accomplish something sooner or later intensifies whatever differences may exist. Typically in Phase 2, the group beings to thrash out *decisions for procedures,* as well as for determining the group's task. Conflict over procedures may be one way in which group members fight for influence or control in the group. The conflict experienced in the group regarding procedures turns out to be very productive for the group in the long run.

Phase 3 involves a *resolution of the conflict* experienced in Phase 2. *Group cohesiveness* begins to emerge, and the group settles into working more confortably as a unit. Open expression of opinions.

Phase 4 is the phase of maximum productivity and *consensus.* Dissent has just about disappeared, and the rule of the moment is to pat each other on the back for having accomplished such a good job. Group members joke and laugh and generally reinforce each other for having contributed to the group's success.

The amount of time spent on each of the phases of group development may vary greatly from group to group.

## TENSIONS AMONG MEMBERS

All of us have experienced many moments of high tension. We feel nervous, irritable, tight, pressured, and strained. Just as individuals experience varying levels of tension, so do entire groups, with virtually every member keyed up and contributing to a high level of performance, bogged down in apathy, or feeling strained and uncomfortable. Of course, the tension is experienced by the individual members; but when all simultaneously experience levels of tension that detract from efficient performance, we have a group tension problem.

Primary tension. Social unease and stiffness that accompanies getting acquainted.

## Helping Roles

Individuals within groups play roles—the individual behavior each member exhibits. A particular style is not intrinsically good or bad. The key is whether or not it is appropriate to the situation.

## Helping Role Categories

1. Establishing. Start the group along new paths. Goals, defines problems, helps set rules, contributes ideas.
2. Establishing indicators
   a. Getting started. Initiating action, suggesting roles, structure or procedures for the group to use.
   b. Clarifying purpose. Stating why the group has been called together. Ensuring commonality of the intended result.
   c. Defining goals. Specifying what is needed to fulfill the group's purpose. Purpose attainment.
   d. Maintaining direction. Keeping the group on track, focusing on the stated goals and purpose.
3. Persuading. Requests the facts and relevant information on the problem. Seeks out expressions of feelings and values. Asks for suggestions, estimates, and ideas. Responds openly and freely to others. Encourages and accepts contributions of others, whether expressed orally or nonverbally.
4. Persuading Indicators
   a. Questioning. Asking questions for the sake of clarity and shared understanding of a point.
   b. Encouraging and guiding responses. It isn't sufficient to ask good questions. It is also people's willingness to respond that helps surface information and insights into their feelings and values.
   c. Developing alternatives. Creating options, coming up with various interpretations, or multiple conclusions, or strategies for consideration.
5. Committing. Helps to ensure that all members are part of the decision-making process. Shows relationships between ideas. May restate suggestions to pull them together. Summarizes and offers potential decisions for the group to accept or reject, reconcile disagreements, open communication channels by reducing tension and getting people to explore differences.
6. Committing Indicators
   a. Facilitating involvement. Making sure people are getting enough air time to provide input.
   b. Synthesizing/Summarizing. Taking a variety of inputs and putting them into a new idea.
   c. Gaining commitment. Tapping into the group to ensure members are on board and buying into the group's progress or results.

    d. Problem solving. Dealing with problems that affect group commitment near the point of implementation. If there is skepticism, offer proof. If there is misunderstanding, a drawback, be creative; procrastination, create a sense of urgency.

7. Attending. Listens, as well as speaks. Easy to talk to. Encourages input from group members and tries to understand, as well as be understood. Takes time to listen and avoids interrupting.

8. Attending Skills
    a. Listening. Remaining silent, maintaining eye contact, and paying attention to what is being said for the purpose of understanding.
    b. Showing interest. Communicating in a way that shows one is involved in the group's process and concerned with its workings; e.g., leaning forward, concentrating on discussion.
    c. Taking notes. Keeping some form of registered evidence of the group's inputs, activities, and decisions that will make them accessible at a later point.
    d. Monitoring or observing. Auditing or examining the group. Paying special attention to the impact things have on the group's process or performance.

## Private Learning

Learning occurs in all types of groups and some join groups for personal enlightenment and growth of their members

    Learning is much more than the acquisition of factual information and skills.
    Change happens because of experience
    Education—structure situations in which the change will be facilitated.

## Learning Objectives

1. Cognitive or intellectual—recognition and recall
2. Affective—having to do with values and feelings
3. Psychomotor—physical skills

## GUIDELINES FOR LEADING PRIVATE LEARNING DISCUSSIONS

1. Always establish a cooperative goal, sharing individual knowledge and thinking.
2. Give rewards to the group, not to individual members.
3. Keep the focus on common experience, reading the same articles or books.

4. Limit the number of issues or topics; jumping from topic to topic should be avoided.
5. Plan a variety of open-ended questions; avoid yes/no questions.

## Types of General Questions

  a. Translation—asking the discussants to change information or statements into their own language.
  b. Interpretation—relationships among facts, generalizations, values, etc.
  c. Analysis—The group is called on to divide an issue or problem into major components or contributing causes.
  d. Value—goodness, rightness or appropriateness.
  e. Prediction—Use information in predicting some future trend or condition.
  f. Synthesis or problem solving—incorporating information.
6. Be guided by the nature of the subject.
7. Focus on how the subject relates to interests of the members of the group.
8. Don't confuse pseudo discussion with a cooperative learning discussion. Be honest. Present yourself in the role of one who has the answers. Each person has perceptions, feelings, interpretations, and ideas about the shared subject matter which should be expressed, understood by other members, elaborated, and perhaps evaluated by the group.

## ORGANIZING LEARNING DISCUSSIONS

1. Topical or Major Issues. Group selects topics or issues, each of which can be phrased as a question. The leader should never insist that the group discuss all or only the leader's questions. The group must decide what issues will be discussed.
2. Comparison. Compare two or more policies, objectives, organizations, etc. for their advantages and disadvantages.
3. Other sequences. Other logical sequences can be employed for arranging major questions raised during learning discussions. Chronological sequence of questions. Any logical sequence with which discussants are familiar could be used to structure a discussion.

## TECHNIQUES FOR LEARNING GROUPS CONCERNED WITH FEELINGS AND INTERPERSONAL RELATIONS

1. Affective discussion. Used to ventilate feelings (Epstein). The technique can be adapted to any learning group at any age level where fears, suspi-

cions, prejudices, and other negative feelings interfere with productive thinking, communicating and relating to other persons.

The purpose of an affective discussion is to help persons express and explore strong feelings which interfere with their ability to make objective, rational responses to factual information, mathematics, public speaking, ideas, food habits, cultural practices, or people different from themselves.

An affective discussion begins with the beliefs that all persons have feelings and that any feeling is all right to have. Affective discussions facilitate expression and empathic listening.

2. Encounter discussion. Personal growth and improving interpersonal relations for the participants. Encounter means that members of the learning group explore their reactions to each other, describing openly and honestly what they feel. Encounter can greatly expand the area of free communication among group members.

## THE SMALL GROUP AS A SYSTEM

Why should we study how small groups work? The better you understand how something works, the more control you are able to exercise so that it becomes productive for you. The more you understand small groups, the more effective you can make your role in the many discussions of which you will be a part.

### The Participant-Observer Perspective

The participant-observer is a regular member of the group, engaging actively in its deliberations, but who, at the same time, is observing, evaluating, and adapting to its processes and procedures.

A participant-observer directs part of his or her attention to participating in the group and part to studying how the group is functioning, trying always to be aware of what the group needs at the moment.

This sort of member can supply needed information, ideas, procedural suggestions, and interpersonal communication skills when needed, or seek them from other members of the group who may not realize what is needed at the moment.

Some members of groups are participants in name only. They add almost nothing to the inputs of the group, though they may detract little from its energy and resources. Some members are valuable because of their personal knowledge or skills but have little understanding of process variables in a small group.

## Small Group Evaluation

All groups can profit from careful observation and skillful evaluation. Improvement demands more than mere participation. Simply being in a group or reading about one does not guarantee success. Specific group interactions must be analyzed.

Feedback regarding the group and its members can take a variety of forms. Evaluations may be oral or written. The members themselves may judge their performance and that of the group. On many occasions, outside observers can watch the group and supply critical comments. What is important in all of these procedures is that members of the group are receiving feedback about their strengths and weaknesses.

Constructive evaluation depends on observation and feedback of information about how a discussion group is doing. Evaluative feedback can be used by the group to change or correct any lack of information, attitudes, norms, or procedures which keep the group from being as productive as it might be.

## THE ROLE OF THE OBSERVER

Every student of discussion and group processes needs the experience of observing discussion groups at work. "It looks different when you are sitting outside the discussion." After observing other discussants, one may be motivated to change his or her own conduct as a discussant. It is therefore suggested that one should observe as many discussions as possible.

No observer can simultaneously chronicle the content and flow of interaction, take note of various group and individual objectives, judge the information and logic of remarks, assess the atmosphere and note the organization of the discussion. If the observer tries to do so, the result is sure to be confusion which will reduce both his or her personal learning and his or her ability to give feedback to the group.

The non participating observer can do three types of things, sometimes all during a single discussion:

1. Learn from the examples of others
2. Remind the group of techniques or principles of discussion they have overlooked
3. Supply critical evaluations of the discussion

## THE REMINDER-OBSERVER

Often group members need to be reminded of what they already know. The reminder helps the group without offering any criticism. Before serving as a reminder, the following guidelines for reminder-observers should be studied carefully. They are designed to reduce defensive reactions to your observations.

1. Stress the positive, pointing out what the group is doing well.
2. Emphasize what is most important, rather than commenting on everything you may have observed.
3. Focus on the processes of the group, rather than on the content and issues *per se*.
4. Don't play the critic-umpire, telling anyone he or she is wrong.
5. Don't argue with a member of the group. If your question is ignored, drop it.
6. Don't tell the group what they should do. You are not playing expert or consultant. Your only job is to remind the group members of what they knew but have overlooked.

## A Checklist for Observing

1. Are the group goals clear? What helped or hindered in clarifying them?
2. Are all members aware of their area of freedom?
3. Is the group gathering information to define the problem fully, or has it become solution-centered too soon?
4. Do members seem to be prepared for discussing the topic?
5. Is information being accepted at face value or tested for dependability?
6. Has a plan for the discussion been worked out and accepted by the group?
7. Does the discussion seem to be orderly and organized?
8. Discussants display attitudes of inquiry and objectivity toward information, issues, and the subject as a whole?
9. To what degree does the climate seem to be one of mutual respect, trust and cohesiveness?
10. Do all members have an equal opportunity to participate?
11. Is the pattern of interaction open, or unduly restricted?
12. How sound is the reasoning being done by the group?
13. How creative is the group in finding potential solutions?
14. Is judgment deferred until all possible solutions can be listed and understood?
15. Does the group have a list of specific and useful criteria, and is it applying them to possible solutions?
16. While evaluating ideas, is the group making use of information from earlier parts of the discussion?
17. Are periodic summaries being used to help members recall and move on to new issues without undue redundancy?
18. Are there any hidden agendas hampering the group?
19. Are there any norms of procedures hampering the group?

20. Are there any breakdowns in communication because of poor listening, bypassing?
21. Is the style of leadership appropriate to the group?
22. If a designated leader is present, is he or she encouraging the sharing of leadership by other members?
23. Is the degree of formality appropriate to group size and task?

A reminder-observer may be able to help the group by leading a discussion of the discussion by making a detailed report of his or her observations.

## THE CRITIC-OBSERVER

A critic-observer may do considerable reminding, but his or her primary function is as a critic. In some cases, the critic-observer is primarily an advisor, either to the group as a whole or to a designated leader. The critic-observer usually makes a more detailed report after the discussion than does the reminder-observer. Discussants can be helped to give and accept criticism by reminding them of two points: (1) All criticism should be constructive, objective, sincere, and designed to help; (2) all critiques should include both positive and negative comments, with all the good points presented first.

In general, judgments should cover at least four basic aspects of the discussion:

1. The group product, including how well it has been assessed, how appropriate it seems to the problem, and how well group members support it
2. The group process, including patterns of interaction, decision making, problem solving, and communication
3. The contribution and functional roles of individual members
4. Leadership

## MEETINGS, CONFERENCES, AND WORKSHOPS

Speech—Lecture. A carefully prepared oral presentation of a subject by a qualified individual. Formality—No opportunity for audience participation. Communication in one direction only.

Speech—Forum. A learning method which consists of an organized speech given by a qualified person and a period of open discussion immediately following—two-way communication. In addition to the speaker, there is usually a chairperson to act as moderator during the discussion.

Panel. A group of three to six persons who carry on a purposeful conversation on an assigned topic. Panel members are selected on the basis of previously demonstrated interest and competence in the subject, as well as their ability to verbalize before an audience. Conversation among panel members is started by a moderator, who usually prepares questions in advance which he or she uses to start and sustain the discussion. There is no audience participation in the panel.

Panel—Forum. A panel which is immediately followed by an audience participation period involving free and open discussion by the panel members on questions submitted by the audience. A moderator usually acts as a go-between for panel members and the audience. Questions can be presented directly from the floor by members of the audience, or the questions can be written on cards which are collected and read by the moderator. Sometimes questions are collected from the audience in advance by the moderator.

Symposium. A series of related speeches by two to five persons qualified to speak on different aspects of the same topic or on closely related topics. Speakers do not converse with one another. They make presentations to the audience. A chairperson is usually in charge.

Symposium—Forum. Symposium followed immediately by an audience participation period of free and open discussion. Moderator acts as a go-between for the speakers and audience. Two-way communication.

Group Discussion. Purposeful conversation and deliberation about a topic of mutual interest among six to twenty participants under the guidance of a trained participant called a leader. Maximum opportunity is provided for the individual participant to share his or her ideas and experiences with others.

## IMPROVEMENT: EVALUATING PEOPLE AND GROUPS

Practice without feedback is not likely to be of any instructional value and may even reinforce bad habits. The only way you are likely to improve, either individually or as a group, is to compare your actual group discussion behavior to desired behavior and strive toward that ideal.

There are several general principles which may guide, but do not guarantee effective communicative behavior in group decision making.

1. Be verbally active.
2. Develop communicative skills.
3. Be sensitive to the group process.
4. Commit yourself to the group.
5. Avoid despair or apparent slowness.

6. Confront social problems.
7. Avoid formulaic answers.
8. Be critical.
9. Be creative.
10. Be honest.

## Problem Solving—Dewey's Reflective Thinking

*Purpose*

To gain problem-solving and critical thinking skills through communicating in small groups.

*Procedure*

In 1910 philosopher and educator John Dewey, in his book, *How We Think,* identified the steps most people follow to solve problems. Dewey did not focus specifically on small groups, but the steps he outlined apply to small groups quite effectively. Dewey's process of *reflecting thinking* is particularly useful when applied to small group process. Dewey's reflective thinking process consists of five steps.

1. Identify and define the problem
    Consider the following questions when attempting to identify and define a problem for group or team deliberations.
    a. What is the specific problem the group is concerned about?
    b. Is the question the group is trying to answer clear?
    c. What terms, concepts, or ideas need to be defined?
    d. Who is harmed by the problem?
    e. When do the harmful effects of the problem occur?
2. Analyze the problem
    During the analysis of the phase of group or team problem solving, members need to research and investigate the problem. In analyzing the problem, a group or team may wish to consider the following questions:
    a. What is the history of the problem?
    b. How serious is the problem?
    c. What are the causes of the problem?
    d. What are the effects of the problem?
    e. What are the symptoms of the problem?
    f. What methods does the group or team already have for dealing with the problem?
    g. What are the limitations of those methods?
    h. How much freedom does the group or team have in gathering information and attempting to solve the problem?

i. What are the obstacles that keep the group or team from achieving the goal?

j. Can the problem be divided into sub problems for definition and analysis? Another phase in the analysis step of the reflective-thinking process is to formulate criteria for an acceptable solution. Criteria are the standards or goals for acceptable solutions. In listing criteria for a solution, you may wish to consider the following questions:

    i. What philosophy should the group or team adopt with respect to solving the problem?

    ii. What are the minimum requirements of an acceptable solution?

    iii. Which criteria are most important?

    iv. How should the group use the criteria to evaluate the suggested solutions?

    Sample criteria for a solution may include the following:

    (1) The solution should be inexpensive.

    (2) The solution should be implemented as soon as possible.

    (3) The solution should be agreed on by all the team members.

3. Suggest possible solutions

After a group or team has analyzed a problem and selected criteria for a solution, it should begin to list possible solutions in tentative, hypothetical terms. Many teams suggest a variety of possible solutions without evaluating them.

4. Suggest the best solution(s)

After a team has compiled a list of possible solutions to a problem, the group should be ready to choose the best solution according the criteria listed. The following questions may be helpful in analyzing the proposed solutions:

a. What would be the long-term effects and short-term effects of this solution if it were adopted?

b. Would the solution really solve the problem?

c. Are there any disadvantages to the solution? Do the disadvantages outweigh the advantages?

d. Does the solution conform to the criteria formulated by the group?

e. Should the group modify the criteria?

5. Test and Implement the solution

Team members should be confident that the proposed solution is valid. In essence, the team should be confident that the solution will solve the problem. The team must then determine specifically how the solution can be put into effect. The following questions may be considered:

a. How can the team get public approval and support for its proposed solution?

b. What specific steps are necessary to implement the solution?

c. How can the team evaluate the success of its problem-solving efforts?

6. In trying to apply reflective thinking to group or team problem solving, consider the following:
    i. Clearly identify the problem you are trying to solve.
    ii. Phrase the problem as a question to help guide group or team discussion.
    iii. Don't start suggesting solutions until you have analyzed the problem.
    iv. In the definition and analysis steps of reflective thinking, don't confuse the causes of the problem with its symptoms.
    v. Constantly evaluate your team's problem-solving method.


## SUGGESTED ACTIVITIES

### Group Evaluation Paper

Write a 3–5 page paper about the way your group functioned. Answer the following questions. Give concrete examples from your group's interactions to explain your answers.

1. When you first entered the group, what were your initial impressions of each group member? Did these impressions change? Why or why not?
2. How did the group or group members use the technique of self-disclosure in the group? What were the results?
3. Were the group members sensitive to each other's feedback. Did the group members really "listen" to one another? If not, why not? If yes, what were the results?
4. How did the group plan and prepare for the in-class discussions? Was this planning sufficient? Effective? Why or why not?
5. What roles were assumed by group members? Include yourself. What were the status rankings? How did the roles and status of group members affect the social and task effectiveness of the group?
6. Who emerged as the natural leader of the group? What kind of a leader was he or she? Did the leadership change during the preparation for discussion? If it did, why?
7. Was the group cohesive? Why or why not? What are some examples of cohesive behavior from the group?
8. What were the problem-solving and decision-making techniques used in your group? Were these the most effective means? Why or why not?
9. What implicit and explicit norms did your group have? What effect did these norms have on the operation of the group?
10. When conflict occurred in your group, what was done to resolve it? Were these methods successful or unsuccessful? Why?

**Table 11.2. Content Analysis Chart: Rate the Group According to the Following Statements as to How Well the Group Achieved the Statement. Place a Check Mark on Each Continuum of These Six Statements. These Statements Reflect a Judgment You are Making After Careful Consideration of What was said During the Discussion.**

| | | | |
|---|---|---|---|
| The group used factual information to support key aspects of the discussion of the problem | No facts | Some facts | Many facts |
| The group distinguished among facts, opinions and assumptions | No distinction | Some distinction | Clear distinction |
| The group provided systemic analysis of alternatives, even if the alternative seemed to have little merit. | Ignored some alternatives | Considered most of the alternatives | Considered all of the alternatives |
| The group distinguished between various types of evidence presented. | No distinctions, accepted all evidence equally | Made some distinctions | Considered all alternatives |
| The group thoroughly defined the problem | Little time on the definitions | Some definition aspects were developed | Thorough coverage of the problem |

Observer: Look at your six judgments, then make an overall evaluation about the group's use of content statements to make this discussion productive.
(Poor Contact Use) 1-2-3-4-5-6-7 (Strong Contact Use)

## State the Discussion Question

For the person you are assigned to observe, mark each time he or she says or does something that fits into one of the identified categories. Use back of page for COMMENTS. Note that you are EXPECTED to make comments.

## Task Behaviors

### *Organization*

- starting, steering, summarizing internally
- keeping group "on track"
- keeping records of ideas, information, progress

*Developing and Analyzing Ideas*

- seeking or contributing new ideas and information
- asking for or seeking information when needed
- analyzing information and ideas
- testing assumptions, questioning definitions

## Group Maintenance Behaviors

*Satisfaction*

- soliciting input from all members
- active listening
- reinforcing, supporting others

*Cohesiveness*

- harmonizing ideas, looking for commonalities
- harmonizing different personalities, styles
- reducing tension
- making group sessions pleasant and rewarding

OVER—Make comments to the person you are observing, stating the things he or she does well and identify a MINIMUM of three things she or he could do to improve.

Source: Jannette Muir, George Mason University

*Chapter Twelve*

# Public Communication

"If all my possessions were taken from me with one exception, I would choose to keep the power of speech, for by it, I would soon regain all the rest."

—Daniel Webster

Public speaking is but one of many modes of human communication. We communicate one-on-one, in small groups, and through mass media, as well as in public. Although each context in which we communicate has its own distinguishing features, certain principles of communication apply to all of them. Whether you focus on an intimate conversation between lovers or an informative speech before a class, the process is always transactional. The speech transaction is the simultaneous exchange that occurs between public speakers and their audience.

Public speaking is a form of communication that is both transactional and symbolic. A transactional model of public speaking suggests the process is far more complex. Rather than a linear interaction, public speaking is a simultaneous exchange between the one speaker and the many that form the audience. The basic components of the speech transaction include source, receiver, message, channel, context, and delivery. These interdependent components occur simultaneously.

Public speaking identifies essential elements and processes in the presentation of a message to an audience within a context.

A speaker can be the center of transactions and occupies a more central position. The speaker and the speech are the reason for gatherings. The speaker's knowledge, speech purpose, speaking ability and attitudes must be examined before, during and after the speech.

The message is the purpose in mind. It is important for speakers to organize messages because it is crucial, because an organized message adds clarity and makes it easier for listeners to understand. It is also good to adjust language to audience, the topic and the situation.

The channel is with the idea that public speaking sometimes is mediated. Messages are the signals by the speaker and received by the listener. The channel is the medium that carries the message signals from sender to receiver.

Noise may be physical; physiological, or semantic with examples such as preconceived ideas, wandering thoughts or misunderstood meanings. To reduce noise in public speaking, it's recommended we use language that's precise, with organized thoughts, and continuously reinforce the message.

The audience in public speaking influences listeners in terms of what we say and how we say it. Know your audience by analyzing what they already know.

The context influences speaker, audience, the speech and its effects. The physical context deals with the setting or place. The sociopsychological context deals with the relationship between speaker and audience. The temporal context deals with the nature of time and the sequence of events.

The cultural context deals with beliefs, lifestyles, values, ways of behaving and appeals.

A speaker's delivery can be enlarged conversations as a good speaker speaks in a conversational style, with enthusiasm, in relation to the audience.

The ethics or morality of speech act is an integral part of all public speaking for speaker, audience and critic.

## THE GROWTH AND DEVELOPMENT OF PUBLIC SPEAKING

How might the courses you are taking this semester contribute to your understanding of public speaking and to increasing your public speaking abilities?

Academic Roots—Contributions to Contemporary Public Speaking

Classical Rhetoric—Emphasis on substance; ethical responsibilities of the speaker; using a combination of logical, ethical, and emotional appeals, the strategies of organization.

Literary and rhetorical—Approaches to and standards for evaluation; insights into style and criticism language.

Philosophy—Emphasis on the logical validity of arguments, continuing contribution to ethics.

Public address—Insights into how famous speakers dealt with varied purposes and audiences to achieve desired effects.

Psychology—How language is encoded and decoded and made easier to understand and remember; theories and findings on attitude change; emphasis on speech effects.

General Semantics—Emphasis on using language to describe reality accurately; techniques for avoiding common thinking errors that faulty language usage creates.

Communication theory—Insights on information transmission, the importance of viewing the whole of the communication act, the understanding of such concepts as feedback, noise, channel, and message.

Interpersonal—Transactionalism, emphasis on mutual influence of speaker and Communication audience.

Sociology—Data an audiences', values, opinions, and beliefs and how these influence exposure to and responses to messages.

Anthropology—Insights into the attitudes, beliefs, and values of different cultures and how these influence communications.

Devito, J (2000) The elements of public speaking. New York: Longman, 5

Public speaking is an activity that involves mental and presentational skills which are different from social conversational skills. To be an effective public speaker requires physical coordination, mental concentration, content organization, skills practice, and a great deal of experience.

There are three primary purposes for giving speeches. Speeches can inform, persuade, or entertain. In addition to the three general purposes of public speaking, there are different styles or methods of delivering a speech. The four basic speaking styles or approaches are manuscript, memorized, extemporaneous, and impromptu.

Without the audience, there is no speech, and there is no speaker. The audience is the reason for the speech. Audience analysis is the process that examines the interests, knowledge, attitudes, and demographics of the audience. Analysis of the audience is essential to the entire speech process. Without it, chances of selecting, researching, and presenting an interesting and captivating speech are severely limited.

Over 20,000 years ago, the Greek philosopher Plato said that every speech should have only three parts: an introduction, a body, and a conclusion. An informative speaker faces quite a challenge speaking before an audience. Some audiences are more receptive than others; yet each member of the audience needs to have his or her interest aroused, to understand what the speaker is saying, and to remember the information after the speaker has finished. Any informative talk has three primary goals: to stimulate interest, increase understanding, and assist retention.

Persuasion is the process of trying to convince others to change their beliefs or behavior. Unlike informative speaking, where the goal is the sharing of information, persuasion is aimed at going a step further—changing others. The persuasive purposes are to reinforce an already held belief, change a belief, and motivate to action. In persuasive speaking, the specific purpose or goal statement is called the proposition. The proposition is the desired effect the speaker wants to have on an audience.

Over 2,000 years ago, Aristotle divided all persuasive effort into three categories: ethos, logos and pathos. Ethos is the ethical appeal, or credibility, of the speaker; logos is the logical appeal, and pathos is the emotional appeal.

## Benefits of Public Speaking

Public speaking has many benefits such as:
1. Enhancing personal and social abilities such as self awareness, self confidence and dealing with the fear of communicating. In the US public speaking is seen as a method for climbing up the socioeconomic ladder (Collier and Powell 1990).
2. Public speaking improves academic and career skills. Among these are abilities to:
   Do research efficiently and effectively
   Explain concepts clearly
   Support an argument with the available means of persuasion
   Understand human motivation
   Organize a variety of messages for clarity and persuasiveness
   Present self with confidence and assurance
   Analyze and evaluate the validity of persuasive appeals
3. Public speaking refines general communication abilities by improving competencies:
   Develop a more effective communication style
   Adjust messages to specific listeners
   Give and respond appropriately to criticism
   Develop logical and emotional appeals
   Communicate with credibility
   Improve listening skills
   Organize extended messages
   Refine public speaking abilities with instruction, exposure, feedback and self reflection through learning experiences

Public speaking is one of the most beneficial aspects of an introductory course. What students learn will be of value in a wide variety of situations. By becoming better listeners and critical thinkers, students will be able to evaluate messages and appeals of all kinds. By developing a greater understanding of themselves and others, students will become more sensitive to people and to situations. By improving presentational skills, students become more self-confident and more willing to engage in serious dialogue with others.

The skills of analysis, organization, and effective presentation are increasingly valued in many careers and occupations. As the American economy moves from dominance by manufacturing to dominance by information, communication skills will become even more important.

An even longer-lasting benefit to studying or teaching public speaking is that it will help make students more competent and responsible citizens. Students will be better able to understand issues and controversies in public life, to determine what they think about those issues, and to participate effectively in decisions that matter. Whether in a local community or in a broader public forum, students will find the ability to speak well empowers them to participate competently in making the decisions that will affect them and others.

## SPEAKING TO INFORM

Informative speaking is often equated with teaching an audience to think about something in a new or different way. In order for such thinking to result, some kind of learning must also occur. The learning process, then, must involve changes in the audience's factual beliefs about some topic or issue. Accordingly, an informative speech is defined as a public presentation designed to change audience members' factual beliefs (the way they think) about a topic or an issue.

An informative speech provides new information or helps the audience understand an issue in a different way.

### Goals of Informative Speaking

1. To communicate new and unfamiliar information to an uninformed audience.
2. To extend what the audience already knows.
3. To update old information about a topic or an issue

Informative Speaking—A speaker describing various ways to practice safe sex intends to inform

Persuading Advocates—A speaker who urges her audience to practice safe sex or abstinence intends to persuade.

### Types of Informative Speeches

1. Briefings. Provide recently available information to an audience with a general understanding of the topic. Examples include a business planner presenting a strategic plan to corporate executives; an employee informally updating her boss about a particular project.

2. Lectures. An instructional presentation that typically provides new or additional information about a subject. Good teachers recognize that their lectures are a type of informative speech; they use public speaking skills to make teaching more effective. A lobbyist who talks with a group of students about what it is like to work in politics or a police officer who talks about home safety at a community center are examples of lecturing. Many lectures invite questions and comments from the audience.

3. Demonstration. Is a "how-to" speech that provides information about doing a particular activity or using a specific object. A student who demonstrates card tricks in the classroom or a sales representative who demonstrates the features of a new athletic shoe at a sports equipment trade show are engaging in demonstration.

4. Training Presentation. To teach a concept or instruct how to complete a task with an acceptable degree of accuracy and to conduct a training presentation. The goal of a training presentation is to help the audience learn. A personnel director who describes payroll and benefit procedures to a group of new employees is conducting a training presentation.

## Organizing and Outlining an Informative Speech

It may appear that informing people in any of the ways described can't be all that difficult. After all, it is just a matter of telling people what they need to know. Once they hear it, they will know it. Unfortunately, it is not that simple because an informative speaker often has only one chance to explain, and the audience has only one chance to comprehend.

## A Basic Format for Informing

Introduction. Compel your audience to listen with some kind of attention-getter and a preview of what is to come. Gaining and holding attention is obviously important. Use a dramatic story, a humorous anecdote.

   Body. Should contain three references.

   Conclusion. Wrap it up; keep your concluding remarks brief.

## Strategies for Improving Informational Effectiveness

1. Keep it simple. Your reasoning, illustrations, explanations, and definitions should be brief and easy to understand.

2. Keep it concrete. Avoid abstract explanations.

3. Be repetitive and redundant. To be repetitive means to say something the same way over and over. To be redundant involves explaining something more than once but in slightly different way each time.

4. Elicit active responses. Use dramatic nonverbal gestures. Ask questions.
5. Use familiar and relevant examples.
6. Use transitions and signposts.
   Topic Ideas
   Television talk shows
   Terrorism
   The use of condoms
   Multicultural
   Abortion
   The feminist movement
   Gun Control
   "Just say No" to drugs
   The generation gap
   Teacher-student dating
   Poverty
   Illiteracy
   Drunk Driving
   Sexual harassment
   Cloning
   Immigration

## ORGANIZING YOUR SPEECH MATERIALS

You need to organize your material if the audience is to understand and re-member it. Here are six patterns you might use to organize the body of a speech: time, space, topic, problem-solution, cause-effect, and the motivated sequence.

### Time Pattern

Organizing major issues on the basis of some time or temporal relationship is a popular pattern for informative speeches. Generally, when this pattern is used, the speech is organized into two, three, or four major parts. You might begin with the past and work up to the present or future, or begin with the present or future and work back to the past. You might organize a speech on a child's development of speech and language in a time pattern. Major propositions might look like this:

1. Babbling is the first stage.
2. Lallation is the second stage.
3. Echolalia is the third stage.
4. Communication is the fourth stage.

Most historical topics lend themselves to organization by a time pattern. Events leading to the Civil War, steps toward a college education and the history of the Internet will all yield to temporal patterning.

## Spatial Pattern

Similar to temporal patterning is organizing the main points of a speech on the basis of space. Both temporal and spatial patterns are especially appropriate for informative speeches. Most physical objects fit well into spatial patterns; the structure of a hospital, school, skyscraper, or even a dinosaur might be appropriately described using a spatial pattern. Here a spatial pattern is used in a speech on places to visit in Central America.

1. Your first stop is Guatemala.
2. Your second stop is Honduras.
3. Your third stop is Nicaragua.
4. Your fourth stop is Costa Rica.

## Topical Pattern

The topical pattern divides the speech topic into subtopics or component parts. This pattern is an obvious one for organizing a speech on, for example, the branches of government. Here the divisions are clear:

1. The legislative branch is controlled by Congress.
2. The executive branch is controlled by the President.
3. The judicial branch is controlled by the courts.

Speeches on problems facing the college graduate, great works of literature, and the world's major religions all lend themselves to a topical organizational pattern.

## Problem-Solution Pattern

This pattern presents the main ideas in two main parts: problems and solutions. Let's say you're trying to persuade an audience that home health aides should be given higher salaries and increased benefits. Here a problem-solution pattern might be appropriate. In the first part of the speech, you might discuss some of the problems confronting home health aides: industry luring away the most qualified graduates of the leading universities, many health aides and then propose solutions and show how the solutions will eliminate problems and appeal for action.

# CHECKLIST FOR THE INFORMATIVE SPEECH

Review this list of questions, making sure your informative speech addresses each issue.

1. Topic Selection
2. Is the topic innovative, and does it provide new information?
3. Is the topic interesting to you as the speaker?
4. In selecting the topic, did you examine your personal interests, experiences, and knowledge?
5. Are you repeating information the audience already knows?

## Research

1. Do you have any personal experiences that can serve as primary source material?
2. Are your sources up to date?
3. Are sources credible? (For example, don't use "House and Garden" magazines for medical information or condensed issues for scientific facts.)
4. Do you build credibility with accurate examples, statistics, and testimony?
5. Have you checked details such as events, numbers, dates, and quotations for precision and accuracy?

## Organization

1. Does the speech have a creative introduction with a clear thesis identifying main points of the body?
2. Do you have an organizational plan appropriate to the topic?
3. Do you use external transitions to emphasize main headings and internal transitions to link subordinate ideas?
4. Have you developed an interesting conclusion conveying finality?

## Language

1. Is your language clear, colorful, and concrete?
2. Do images evoke mental pictures which appeal to the senses?
3. Do you avoid trite phrases, jargon, and grammatical errors?

## Supporting Materials

1. Do you humanize the topic with realistic supporting materials?
2. Have you rounded statistics for easy comprehension?

3. Do you employ colorful quotations?
4. Have you avoided stringing long lists of statistics or "hard" facts?
4. Do you have any visual aids in the speech to create interest and variety?

## Delivery

1. Do you refer to your sources in the speech?
2. Do you pronounce difficult names and technical terms correctly?
3. Have you defined difficult words or phrases?
4. Do you use terms the audience can understand?
5. Do you maintain eye contact with the audience?
6. Do you use personal pronouns such as "you," "we," "us"?
7. Are you conversational, avoiding word-for-word delivery?
8. Do you make effective use of the eyes, face, hands, and voice?
9. Do you stimulate feedback by using humor, asking rhetorical questions, and employing emotion?
10. Are you able to make minor adjustments to content or delivery based upon audience response?
11. Have you practiced the speech to gain confidence?

## COMMUNICATION APPREHENSION (CA)

### Definition

"An individual's level of fear or anxiety associated with either real or antici-pated communication with another person or persons." (Mccroskey and Wheeless 1976)

### Types and Causes of Communication Apprehension

*Trait*

May be caused by heredity, environment, negative or mixed reinforcement, housing choices.

*Situational or State*

May be caused by a novel situation, formality, subordinate status, conspic-uousness, unfamiliarity with cultural norms, dissimilarity to others, and too much attention from another constant evaluation, and prior history of failure.

## Signs of Communication Apprehension

*Internal*

Physical discomfort—including flushing, increased heart rate, nausea

*External*

1. Communication avoidance (avoiding situations that require communication)
2. Communication withdrawal (not answering questions, purposefully giving minimal or incorrect responses)
3. Communication disruption (stuttering, avoiding eye contact, biting nails, etc.)

## Effects of Communication Apprehension

On Others' Perceptions
   Competence
   Anxiety
   Assertiveness
   Responsiveness
   Leadership abilities
   Attractiveness
On School
On Work

## Treatment of Communication Apprehension

Effects of High Communication Apprehension on Student Behavior
General Behavior
   Possess low tolerance for disagreement, less self-control
   Possess low tolerance for ambiguity
   Behave less adventurously and innovatively
   Disclose less, lack trust
   Feel tension in classroom setting
   Have lower self-esteem
   Feel isolated

## Specific Behaviors

   Prefer lecture
   Drop high communication courses
   Don't participate in class

Have lower GPA and achievement test scores
May prefer non-central seating

## Treatment of Communication Apprehension

Systematic Desensitization—Learning to relax the body while meditating on high Communication Apprehension situations
Cognitive Restructuring—Substituting coping statement for negative self-statements
Skills Training—Learning public speaking skills, assertiveness training
Visualization

## Classroom Treatment

Offer support and encouragement
Avoid ridicule or criticism of student responses
Use students' first names
Limit class discussion to small classes
Use small group discussion
Provide advance copies of questions
Vary seating arrangements
Let students choose seats
Don't grade class participation
Focus on students, not just on task

## AUDIENCE ANALYSIS SHEET

What is the nature of the speaking occasion?
What is the composition of this audience?
   Size:
   Age:
   Gender:
   Occupation:
   Education:
      Group Memberships:
   Cultural-Ethnic Background:
   What is listeners' knowledge of the subject area?
   What are their general beliefs, attitudes, and values?
      Political:
      Professional:
      Economic:
      Other Pertinent Areas:

What is their general attitude toward me as a speaker?
What is their general attitude toward the speech purpose?
Given this analysis, how should I prepare my presentation?

## Defining Persuasion

Persuasion is the process of changing or reinforcing attitudes, beliefs, values or behavior. To show how persuasion works, several theories of persuasion tell us that listeners may be motivated to respond to the persuasive message.

Cognitive dissonance involves developing a sense of disorganization or imbalance to prompt a person to change when new information conflicts with previously organized thought patterns. Maslow's hierarchy of needs is another approach which attempts to explain why people may be motivated to respond to persuasive messages. Both fear appeals can motivate listeners to respond to persuasive messages. A key to persuading others is to establish credibility that involves an audience's perception of a speaker's competence, trustworthiness and dynamism.

Reasoning is also important in persuasion. Drawing conclusions from evidence is integral to the persuasive process. The types of reasoning are; inductive, deductive and causal.

To become an effective and ethical persuader we should avoid reasoning fallacies such as causal fallacy, bandwagon fallacy, hasty generalization and personal attack.

Throughout the persuasive speech process, be aware of messages and others messages, effectively use verbal and nonverbal messages, listen to your audience and adapt to audience.

## Ten Principles of Persuasion

Principle—Advice.

Selective Exposure—Anticipate selective exposure when you challenge existing attitudes, beliefs, and values.

Cultural Differences—Take into consideration cultural differences placed on persuasive appeals and patterns.

Audience Participation—Actively involve the audience; make them a part of the process.

Inoculation—Strive for small gains with an inoculated audience; proceed inductively when attacking inoculated beliefs; refute counter-arguments when strengthening an audience's beliefs.

Magnitude of Change—Strive for small gains; get your "foot in the door" by beginning with a very small request and leading up to your real request; get the "door in your face" by beginning with a request larger than you really want and following it with a smaller request.

Identification—Establish common ground with the audience; emphasize similarities and points of agreement.

Consistency—Show the audience how their beliefs and values are consistent with what you are urging them to believe or do.

Logos, logical appeals—Use reliable and valid evidence and sound argument to prove your case.

Pathos, motivational—Arouse the emotions of the audience; appeal to the motives that influence their behavior.

Ethos, credibility appeals—Establish your own believability by stressing your competence, character, and charisma.

Devito, J (2000) The elements of public speaking. New York: Longman. 386

## PREPARING A PERSUASIVE SPEECH

Preparing and presenting a persuasive speech requires the same general approach as preparing any kind of speech. In persuasion it is important to select a topic that is of interest to the speaker and the audience. Suggested tips for framing purposes in persuasion involve the formulation of a proposition of fact, value or policy.

Organizing persuasion might include problem solution, cause-effect, refutation, and the motivated sequence. The motivated sequence involves five steps: attention, need, satisfaction, visualization and action.

## STRATEGIES FOR PERSUADING YOUR AUDIENCE

Aristotle (1960) said that rhetoric is the process of discovering all the available means of persuasion. Aristotle singled out strategies for persuading.

Establishing credibility is an audience's perception of a speaker's competence, trustworthiness and dynamism. A speaker should be well informed, skilled and knowledgeable. A speaker in delivering a speech should convey honesty and sincerity to audience. Dynamism involves effectively using and understanding non verbal messages, maintaining eye contact, being enthusiastic, good vocal inflection, moving and gesturing purposefully. A charismatic speaker possesses charm, talent and other qualities that make the speaker attractive and energetic.

# PERSUASIVE PROJECT ASSIGNMENT

This project requires you to (1) plan for; (2) actually attempt to persuade some person (several people) in a "real," outside-of-class situation; (3) evaluate what happened and why and (4) report on all of these in a typed, 5–10 page paper, of which one copy is to be turned in to your instructor accompanied by the evaluation form on the date indicated on the daily schedule. This should be a paper, not merely an outline, though the outline below could provide a strong framework for the paper.

Read the assignment guidelines carefully and be sure to clarify any requirements you do not understand. Following the assignment is a sample evaluation form and a discussion of criteria your instructor will follow in evaluating this project.

In choosing your goal for the project, keep in mind that this project will be evaluated by what your report shows that you know about the persuasion process; it will not be evaluated by whether or not you succeed at achieving the goal.

## Directions

1. Establish a behavioral goal
   a. Choose the goal.
   Select a specific persuasive outcome (outside this class) you would like to achieve, a goal that is real and (hopefully) important to you. This is to be a specific action that you seek from someone, or a group of people.
   Select a significant goal. Do not choose a simplistic task just because this is an "assignment." Success is not what counts for the assignment.
   b. State the goal in behavioral terms. State who is to do what, when and under what circumstances. In other words, identify what your receiver(s) will say, do, think, or feel, if you are successful.
   c. Show your goal statement to your instructor to be sure it is specific and appropriate for the assignment. Secure this approval before proceeding.

Next, work methodically through the planning steps outlined under Roman numeral I in the outline below. When your planning is complete, attempt the persuasion as planned, evaluate what happened, and write your paper.
*Outline for Planning and Evaluating Persuasive Efforts:*
*NOTE: Secure instructor approval of item I before proceeding.*

2. Planning
   This is one of the two most important parts of this project. It should involve at least the following:
   a. Analyze your receiver(s). This means, at the least, answer the following questions:
      i. What specific things do I know about the receiver(s) that will help me to infer their attitudes relevant to my goal? Or help me decide how to persuade them?
         (1) relevant reference groups
         (2) relevant knowledge of previous experiences
         (3) relevant values, beliefs, feelings
         (4) attitudes about subject and goal
      ii. What relevant receiver attitudes can I infer?
         (1) toward subject?
         (2) toward issues?
         (3) toward me as a persuader?
         (4) attitudes toward the goal?
      iii. How does/do the receiver(s) see my credibility on this particular issue?
      iv. What do you infer the receiver(s) position(s) to be before your persuasive effort?
   b. Analyze your situation, answering at least the following questions:
      i. What is the setting I'll be in? Will anything about time, place, communication climate, environment, relationships among receivers, or other factors affect my persuasive effort?
      ii. Are there other specific barriers I will have to overcome to achieve the desired response?
      iii. What other factors might affect the persuasive effort?
         (1) receiver expectations of me? or relevant others?
         (2) receiver commitments?
   c. Given the preceding analysis, is the goal attainable, either in the short- or long-range?
      i. Having reached this point in analysis, do I need to reassess my goal and continue my planning?
      ii. If so, what is the restated goal?
   d. Plan the persuasive message(s), considering at least the following
      i. How many messages will I need?
      ii. What basic argument(s) will I use?
      iii. How do these arguments relate to persuasion theory?
      iv. What structure will I use?
      v. What motive appeal(s) will I use
      vi. To improve my credibility, I will:
      vii. I'll overcome the identified barriers by:

3. Implementation

Conduct your persuasive effort. Remember to make notes immediately so that you can recall accurately what happened.

4. Evaluation and Analysis

Evaluate the persuasive effort. Think carefully through what happened and why. This is one of the two most important parts of the project. Your analysis should involve answering at least the following questions:

a. How close did I come to achieving my goals? Why did the persuasion work? Or, why didn't it work?

b. What happened that demonstrated my receiver analysis was accurate? Or, inaccurate?

c. What could I have done better?

d. What did I do especially well?

e. What changes would I make if I were able to start over again?

5. Requirements for the paper

Turn in, on time, two copies of a typed (double-spaced) 5–10 page paper, accompanied by the Persuasive Project Evaluation Form from the forms section of this Syllabus and Study Guide. See the daily schedule for due dates. Your project score will be reduced by 10 points for each day the paper is late.

The paper should contain a clear statement of your goal, a concise description of your planning for and execution of the persuasive effort, and include a significant degree of analysis and evaluation of the entire effort. To repeat, whether or not your persuasion was successful is unimportant. What is important is that you demonstrate an understanding of the persuasive process.

Remember, once you have specified your goal and secured approval of it, the important part of this assignment is analysis—the planning and evaluation of what happened. You briefly describe what you did and what happened only to provide the basis for the person who reads your paper to understand your analysis.

Remember, you may turn in your outline and draft of the report in advance of the due date for early feedback from your instructor to improve your final paper. See the daily schedule for deadlines.

## PERSUASIVE PROJECT EVALUATION CRITERIA

1. A paper does not meet minimum criteria unless it

a. identifies specifically who is to do what

b. addresses receiver analysis and adaptation in describing the planning for the effort

c. reports briefly what happened

d. discusses why the effort succeeded or failed

2. Quality assessments will be based on whether
   a. The goal also specified when the desired action is to occur and under what conditions.
   b. The planning fully addresses the important issues to be considered in persuasion and relates appropriate material from the text and assigned readings.
   c. The report of what happened is complete, yet concise.
   d. The evaluation of what was done and analysis of what happened is thorough and insightful, reflecting an understanding of the readings about persuasion assigned in this unit.
3. Deductions from quality ratings will be made for papers that do not reflect college-level writing—that is, for:
   a. papers with mechanical errors in spelling (typographical errors are spelling errors; proofread carefully), grammar, punctuation, etc. A point will be deducted for each such error minus one that the paper contains.
   b. papers that are poorly organized, unclear, incoherent

## MINIMUM CRITERIA FOR AN ACCEPTABLE SPEECH

Students must meet minimum standards in Parts A, B, and C. If these standards are met, point total for the speech is obtained by adding total points for all four parts.

### Part A: Achieved Appropriate Listener Understanding

70 per cent average accuracy achieved by Listeners

### Part B: Followed Assignment Directions

1. The speech gives listeners new information or new insights.
2. The speech was on a significant topic.
3. The speech was not a "how to" speech.
4. An appropriate visual aid was used.
5. Three specific outside references cited, in sufficient detail to locate sources.
6. The speech was at least 6 minutes long, not more than 10.

### Part C: Speaker Achieved Minimum Presentation Standards

1. Speaker conveyed a sincere desire that listeners understand an important idea.

**Table 12.1. Persuasive Project Evaluation Form**

MINIMUM CRITERIA:

Acceptable  Not acceptable

_____   _____   Goal statement identifies who is to do what
_____   _____   Planning addresses issues of audience analysis and adaptation
_____   _____   A brief report of what happened is given
_____   _____   Evaluation/Analysis addressed why success or failure occurred

Points earned from minimum criteria:

_____   Unless all of the above are marked acceptable, the maximum points a paper may earn is 50 points (Additional points may be deleted for poor grammar or other mechanical errors).

QUALITY RATING—If the above criteria are satisfied, the second section shall serve as a guide for quality assessment.

KEY:   Superior = 5   Very Good = 4   Acceptable = 3   Fair = 2   Poor = 1

Ratings   Total Points

_____ (x 1) = _____   Goal statement identifies when and under what conditions the what is to occur
_____ (x 1) = _____   Planning fully addresses questions raised in assignment
_____ (x 1) = _____   Report of what happened is concise, yet complete
_____ (x 1) = _____   Evaluation/Analysis of why persuasive effort was or was not successful is insightful and thorough

Total Quality Points:
_____ Met Minimum Criteria
_____ Subtotal
_____ Minus for Mechanical Errors
_____ Minus for lateness (10 points per day late)
_____ TOTAL POINTS (100 possible)

2. Speaker maintained reasonable eye contact with listeners.
3. S/he spoke extemporaneously, using 3 or fewer 4 x 6 notes cards.

If all checked (all 10), add 20 points.

## Selected Passages for Practice in Vocal Expression

Oral reading is one of the easiest and most commonly used methods of improving vocal expression. Oral reading is more, however, than just reading aloud. It is reading in such a manner as to express the ideas of the author. A good oral reader, therefore, prepares him or her self by (1) studying the

**Table 12.2.    Informative Speech—Evaluation Form**

Speaker:
Critic:
Thesis Statement:

Introduction:                                        Comments:
_____ gained attention/interest
_____ introduced topic clearly,
        prepared audience
        for speech
_____ Identified with audience
Body:
_____ organization well planned
_____ main points are clear
_____ transitions are strong
_____ arguments supported with evidence
        or good examples
Conclusion:
_____ tied points together
_____ left strong impact
Delivery:
_____ relaxed and confident
_____ few vocal fillers
_____ language use appropriate
_____ direct eye contact with audience
_____ use of gestures, movement
_____ enthusiasm for topic
_____ vocal dynamics
Overall:
_____ topic challenging
_____ specific purpose well chosen
_____ maintained time constraints
_____ offered a new, different view

TOTAL POINTS _____

INFORMATIVE SPEECH EVALUATION FORM
DATE _____            _____ First Speech
                                       _____ First redo
SPEAKER: _____            _____ Redo # ___
RATER: _____            _____ Mastery Achieved
                                       _____ Point Total

selection until they understand the meanings and feelings of the author, (2)
practicing word or thought grouping until expressing ideas in a clear and
understandable manner, (3) using pauses effectively for emphasis, and (4)
regulating the rate of reading to suit the size of the audience and to bring
out the meaning and mood of material.

Before beginning your practice on any one passage, study it carefully to understand its full meaning and allow yourself to drink in the dominant mood. Avoid mere superficial and manipulation of voice; read so as to make the meaning clear and feeling contagious to your listeners. Effective reading of this sort requires enough practice in private so that before an audience you will not need to think of vocal skills but can concentrate on the ideas and feelings you are trying to express.

## 1. One Idea

If I had a choice given me of one idea or all the atomic bombs in existence, I'd unhesitatingly choose the one idea. You would too. If you don't think so, then let's look closely at some ideas.

For instance, Henry Ford just had one idea. His idea was to produce a car cheap enough so that the man in the street, the common man, could afford to buy it. If you look in the files of almost any newspaper from September 1922, you will find advertised there a Ford chassis and motor delivered complete for $290 and a five passenger touring car complete and ready to go for $450.

We Americans paid Henry Ford more than a billion dollars for his one idea. And we got our money's worth.

## 2. From the 19th Chapter of First Kings

And, behold, the Lord passed by, and a great and strong wind rent the mountains, and brake in pieces the rock before the Lord; but the Lord was not in the wind; and after the wind an earthquake; but the Lord was not in the earthquake; and after the earthquake a fire; but the Lord was not in the fire; and after the fire a still, small voice.

## 3. Liberty or Death

There is no retreat but in submission and slavery! Our chains are forged. Their clanking may be heard on the plains of Boston! The war is inevitable- and let it come! I repeat it, sir, let it come! It is vain, sir, to extenuate the matter. Gentlemen may cry peace, peace—but there is no peace. The war has actually begun. I know not what course others may take; but, as for me, give me liberty, or give me death!

## 4. Life on the Mississippi

I'm the original iron-jawed, brass-mounted, copper-bellied, corpse-maker from the wilds of Arkansas! Look at me! I'm the man they call Sudden Death and General Desolation! Sired by a Hurricane, dam'd by an earthquake, half-brother to the cholera, nearly related to the small-pox on the mother's side! Look at me! I take nineteen alligators and a bar'l of whiskey for breakfast when I'm in robust health and a dead body when I'm ailing! I split the everlasting rocks with my glance, and I quench the thunder when I speak! Who-oop!

## 5. Blood, Toil, Sweat and Tears

I have nothing to offer but blood, toil, sweat and tears. We have before us an ordeal of the most grievous kind.

What is our policy? I say it is to wage war by land, sea and air. War with all our might and with all the strength God has given us, and to wage against a monstrous tyranny never surpassed in the dark and lamentable catalogue of human crime.

What is our aim? I can answer in one word. VICTORY! Victory at all costs-victory in spite of all terrors-victory however long and hard the road may be, for without victory there is no survival.

6. Westinghouse Commercial

Do you want numerous gadgets on your new TV set? If not, buy Westinghouse. Simple one-dial tuning. Westinghouse electric viewing gives you the clearest picture. For free demonstration call your local Westinghouse dealer. Remember, you can be sure if it's Westinghouse.

7. Ivory Commercial

I can't say this often enough. It's so true! Your hands can have "That Ivory look" in just twelve days. Do you think washing dishes brings red Knuckles, catchy fingertips and coarse skin? Then learn this: It can come from using the wrong soap! If that's the case with you, your hands can have "that Ivory Look" in just twelve days. Y'know doctors advise Ivory soap for skin-care over any other soap. Naturally, "skin-care" includes the hands.

8. To Develop Enthusiasm

Boy! Look at that boat. She's a beauty!

That's the most magnificent sunset I have ever seen.

Why don't you come with us? Come on. We'll have a wonderful time.

I'm very glad to meet you. This is a pleasure. I'm delighted.

I hope to see you soon again.

Hey! What a drive! Wish I could hit the ball like you do, Harry.

Promise? Will you really do it? Oh, that's great!

I must say, I'm very proud of you.

It's just what I wanted. You couldn't have picked a nicer gift.

It's marvelous, marvelous! A true miracle.

## Chapter Thirteen

# Freedom of Speech

Almost every profession has its code of ethics. Doctors, lawyers, broadcasters, journalists, teachers all have established standards of ethical conduct. That is not to say that everyone in each of these professions abides by the standards to the letter. There is no force of law that compels them to do so, only their own sense of moral obligation and regard for their professional reputation. Schools, colleges, and universities require that graduates have an understanding of ethical standards in their field of study in order to maintain the historical tradition and the integrity of the profession.

Freedom to speak and responsibility in public speaking work together for the social good in a democratic society. Both are derived from our democratic values, which include respect for the individual as a person of dignity, worth and critical capacity. The assumptions of democracy that flow from respect for persons include preference for persuasion over force as a means of change, the right for free speech, decision by majority vote, and regard for minority rights.

Although speakers in the United States have almost unlimited liberty to address any subject of concern, some restrictions do apply, as set forth by the courts over the years. First, concerning speech content, speaking on political and social issues, including criticism of the government, is permitted until it reaches the point of inciting an audience to illegal conduct in those circumstances in which the audience is likely to carry out that conduct. In addition, defamatory falsehoods (slander and libel) are not protected by the constitution: such expression invites civil suits for monetary damages, especially when a person falsely accuses another of such things as criminality, disease, dishonesty, or sexual immorality. However, one is protected from government action when you discuss or criticize religion, for the Supreme Court has ruled that the state has no "legitimate interest in protecting any or all religions from views distasteful to them"

Second, reasonable regulations of time, place, and manner are permitted, especially as applies to parades, marches, and demonstrations. Rules that require securing a parade permit in advance of an event are allowed by the courts, provided the issuing agency administers the permit system without picking and choosing from among applicants (that is, without "discretion"). In short, permits must be given in a way that is equitable to all.

Third, the U.S. Supreme Court has been supportive of freedom of speech on the college campus, including academic freedom, although some restrictions do apply. In general, students and faculty members in public colleges and universities (but not necessarily in private ones) have the same liberty of expression while on campus as they do off the campus. However, this liberty should be exercised on campus so as not to interfere with or disrupt the educational process.

In addition to communication freedom, the speaker in a democracy has at least four key areas of *communication responsibility:* (1) to himself or herself; (2) to the audience; (3) to the content of the speech; and (4) to society at large. The personal responsibility means that the speaker should be prepared, knowledgeable, and sincere. In addition, the audience should be approached with an attitude of respect. Speech content should be founded in reason, and should be supported by sound evidence. Finally, the speaker should be concerned with the social consequences of the message.

In his discussion of the *Ethics of Speech Communication,* Professor Thomas R. Nilsen of the University of Washington summarizes well the theme of this chapter. Writes Nilsen:

In public discourse the speech that serves our values is that which strengthens the processes of democracy, fosters freedom of expression, provides information adequate for constructive decisions, engages in significant debate, examines alternatives and objectively appraises evidence and conclusions, and inspires to noble objectives. This includes truth telling.

## HISTORY OF FREE SPEECH IN THE U.S.

1791—First Amendment to the U.S. Constitution guarantees that Congress shall make no law bridging freedom of speech.

1798—Sedition Act passes.

1919—Supreme Court suggests that speech presenting a "clear and present danger" may be restricted.

1920—American Civil Liberties Union is formed.

1940—Congress declares it illegal to urge the violent overthrow of the federal government.

1964—Berkeley Free Speech Movement takes place.

1966—Supreme Court forces Georgia to seat Julian Bond, who spoke publicly in support of draft resistance.

1989—Supreme Court defends the burning of the U.S. flag as a speech act.

1995—Supreme Court hands down eight free speech rulings in first six months of term.

What does freedom of speech mean?

In 1972 the Speech Communication Association adopted a credo for free and responsible communication in a democratic society. It condemns physical and coercive interference in the free speech of others. It urges respect for accuracy in communication and for reasoning based on evidence. Although the ability to speak in public is not something that requires a license or a degree, it is a recognized academic discipline, and students who choose to study the art at the college or university level should have the same appreciation for a code of ethics the people who pursue professional careers have.

1. You can speak freely without fear of retaliation.
2. You can expose yourself freely to all sides of a controversial issue.
3. You can debate freely all disputable questions of fact, value, or policy.
4. You can make decisions freely based on your evaluation of the choices confronting you.

The First Amendment protects citizens' right to speak freely. Unless others listen to what is being said, the right becomes an empty right. An important dimension of the First Amendment is that we also have the right to listen, if we will, and to evaluate what we hear. What free speech means is that we will be exposed to all kinds of viewpoints. We will hear false information, as well as the truth, and we must learn to separate one from the other.

Expression of ideas whether they are popular or unpopular

Ideas we support or oppose

Ideas we feel deeply committed to or don't care about

Ideas we believe must be accepted

The right to freedom of expression requires that we exercise our ears and listen carefully and critically to what others have to say

## DEMOCRATIC VALUES: THE FOUNDATION FOR FREE AND RESPONSIBLE SPEAKING

In order to locate the basic democratic principles upon which free and responsible speaking are built, we will examine two key topics. First we will discuss the tenet of respect for the individual, and second, we will look at some operational assumptions about democracy that flow from our respect for persons.

### The Value of the Individual

Our society believes in the value of each person. This belief is often expanded and supported by three concepts about persons: individual dignity and worth; capacity to reason; and equality. Let us note each of these briefly.

### Individual Dignity and Worth

Because we believe that each person has dignity and worth, we stress that our institutions, including those of government, should serve the people, and not the other way around. It follows from this democratic perspective that public speakers, being persons of worth, should be accorded a courteous hearing, even if we, as members of the audience, disagree with them. Also, it follows that speakers should avoid the "know-it-all," authoritarian language that insults listeners, and instead, demonstrate respect for the individuals who compose the audience.

### *Capacity to Reason*

We believe that each person of normal intelligence has the capacity for rational thought and intelligent decision making. This tenet of democracy gives us an additional reason for listening courteously when we are an audience member, or as a speaker, approaching our audience with respect, for we accept the view that both speakers and listeners are capable of thinking an issue through and reaching a sensible conclusion about it.

### *Equality*

We also believe in the right of each person to participate equally in society. This includes equal participation in the institutions of self-government. Education in public speaking serves this value, for it enables citizens to take part in democratic discussion and debate on an equal footing. Even though we recognize that abilities vary from person to person, we try to provide the same opportunities to all. This ideal was stated eloquently by Thomas Jefferson in the Declaration of Independence: "We hold these truths to be self-evident, that all men are created equal, that they are endowed by their Creator with certain unalienable Rights that among these are Life, Liberty, and the pursuit of happiness."

## Assumptions of Democracy

At least four assumptions of democracy flow from our beliefs in individual worth, capacity, and equality. These are a preference for persuasion over force, freedom of speech so that persuasion can take place, decision by majority vote, and respect for minority rights.

### Preference for Persuasion

Persuasion is a civilized, non violent means of achieving political and social change. Even though changes brought about by persuasion are usually evolutionary rather than revolutionary, we prefer it to the alternatives of coercion and force.

### Freedom of Speech

For persuasion to be effective, individuals must have freedom to communicate and to receive information and opinion communicated by others. As Yale Law Professor Thomas I. Emerson observes in *The System of Freedom of Expression,* "By its very nature a system of free expression involves in fact is designed to achieve persuasion. . .The introduction of coercion destroys the system as a free one." By practicing liberty of speech, we hope to keep viable a "marketplace of ideas" that supplies citizens of a free society with essential information and a variety of points of view.

### Decision by Majority Vote

After the members of a group, or the citizens of a democratic society, are "made wise" by free, vigorous discussion and debate on the issues in question, a vote is taken. The decision of the majority prevails.

### Respect for Minority Rights

Within the context of majority rule, certain fundamental rights are protected for the minority. In the United States, a number of these rights are set forth in the federal Constitution, and include such important matters as freedom to communicate, freedom of religion, protection from arbitrary search and seizure, and the right of an accused person to a fair trial.

We are now ready to apply the basic values and assumptions of democracy to your right of free speech and to the formulation of ethical standards for public communication in a free society.


## SPEAKING FREELY: LEGAL ISSUES
## FOR THE PUBLIC SPEAKER

The First Amendment to the U. S. Constitution states:

Congress shall make no law respecting an establishment of religion, or prohibiting the free exercise thereof; or abridging the freedom of speech, or of the press; or the right of the people peaceably to assemble, and to petition the Government for a redress of grievances.

In 1925, the U. S. Supreme Court ruled that the First amendment is binding on the governments of the states as well as upon the federal government. In other words, neither the federal nor the state governments may deny us freedom of speech or of the press.

Freedom of speech, however, is not an absolute, not in the United States, and not in other democratic societies, ancient or modern. Both Athens and Rome, for example, punished slander (that is, spoken accusations that tend to destroy a person's good reputation) and sedition (undermining the democracy by extreme form of criticism).

Furthermore, not all speech that is protected by the constitution is ethical. Just because speech is permitted does not mean that what results is always based on sound reasoning, solid evidence, a commitment to truth, and a sense of social responsibility. Public speakers, then, need to be aware of two areas of concern: the legal controls applied to public communication in the United States, and the standards of communication ethics that speakers should follow when addressing their fellow citizens.

In the United States, the language of the constitution is open to interpretation by the courts, especially the U.S Supreme Court which has the final word on the judiciary's views of the constitution. Although the Supreme Court has interpreted the First Amendment to mean that most speech is protected, it has also said that some speech (such as false advertising) is not. College speech students should be familiar with the way the courts have ruled in at least three areas of public communication: controls upon the content of speech; the regulation of expression involving parades, marches, or demonstrations; and freedom of speech on the campus.


### Controls Upon Speech Content

There are three major issues of speech content that you should be aware of as you plan your speeches. They concern criticism of the government (sedition), defamation of individuals (slander and libel), and criticism of religion (blasphemy).

## COMMUNICATION AND ETHICS

The historical development of freedom of speech and ethics forces certain issues into our consciousness. Historical perspectives on the development of free speech with the passage of years can be interpreted and reinterpreted by looking at freedom of speech in ancient Greece, Rome, England, and the United States; and one can comment on the thematic legal and ethical patterns surrounding the issues of free speech.

Free speech issues are worthy of concern, and they arise in human behavior whenever that behavior involves conscious choice of means and ends and when the behavior can be judged by standards of right and wrong.

In ancient Athens, around 800–600 BC, aristocratic rulers permitted certain classes of citizens to express their opinions without fear. Such citizens were thought of as bright, honest, and socially responsible. Athens had such a reputation for personal freedom that artists, philosophers, teachers and statesmen were drawn from afar to the creative ferment of the remarkable city states to participate in the democratic process.

However, the liberty in Athens was not absolute, for its exercise was reserved for adult male citizens. Juveniles, women, and resident aliens were not considered "citizens", and did not therefore have a right to free speech. Restricting free speech were traditions or laws against slander (speaking evil of others), impious speech (blasphemy of the sacred), and sedition (severe criticism of the government).

Like Athens, Rome permitted a high degree of freedom of speech. However, the stronger influences were on responsibility. Laws and traditions against personal slander were well documented. Rome had legal restrictions against extreme forms of political criticism, such as sedition.

The signing of the *Magna Carta* by King John in 1215 A.D. created documentation of what is now recognized as the foundation of constitutional liberty for both England and the United States. The *Magna Carta* planted significant seeds of liberty by declaring that justice was not to be sold, denied, or delayed and that no free person could be deprived of life or property except by peer judgment and by the law of the land.

The *Magna Carta* gave support to the evolution of liberty, including freedom of speech. The powers of church and state in England managed for centuries to restrain the development of liberty by imposing controls upon public communication, such as controls on communicators by king and clergy. The adoption of the writ of *habeas corpus* provided protection from arbitrary arrest and imprisonment of those persons who were the originators of unpopular opinions.

In the United States, with the ratification of the Bill of Rights in 1791, freedom of speech for all its citizens became official public policy. Despite this law, the four libels of English common law were generally accepted in legal circles, resulting in the government actions from time-to-time against speech perceived to be seditious, defamatory, blasphemous, or obscene.

Most First Amendment law under which Americans now live has been molded by the United States Supreme Court since 1919, and this has occurred to a great extent in decisions concerning seditious libel which originated from the landmark case of 1919 in which the clear-and-present-danger test was proposed.

In general, defamation and speech that invades privacy remain outside the protection of the First Amendment. Defamation is speech that tends to lower a person's reputation, cause that person to be shunned, or expose that person to hatred, contempt or ridicule.

Six clearly defined religious-moral offenses of belief and expression emerge from Anglo-American history: teaching false doctrine, blasphemy, profane and disgusting speech, explicit erotic expression, certain opinions and facts of science, and dissenting views concerning private morality.

It is clearly evident that there have been historical transitions of free speech from the Greeks to the Romans, to the English, to the United States. While one could agree that there has been free speech in all these countries, one could also point out that free speech is not absolute. The Greeks gave a selected few the freedom to speak; the Romans had sedition laws; the English gave greater freedom following the signing of the *Magna Carta*; and in the United States, there have been free speech issues such as sedition, defamation, blasphemy, obscenity, and clear and present danger in relation to the First Amendment.

pplicable standards exist to protect and promote the healthiest communication behavior. It is true that freedom is a central principle of accurate interpretation but can be proven somewhat problematic because support of absolute freedom of speech might conflict with other standards.

It is therefore imperative to interpret and judge each communication situation by intent and effect. Asking communicators to accept responsibility for statements they make relates to standards of fairness, objectivity and freedom. When a person seeks to communicate to another person, that communicator carries responsibility to act in keeping with the fairness, objectivity, and freedom doctrines. Legated nature of legal and medium of expression "is a law unto itself".

## DOMINANT AMERICAN VALUES

As Americans we should be familiar with our own value orientations. Since we carry our culture with us wherever we go and in everything we do, our values, an essential part of our culture, play significant roles in our communicative behavior. We should know them and also be familiar with the values of people we meet, especially from other cultures.

In our review of American values, we concentrate on those characteristics of the American macroculture—the prevailing Anglo-Saxon culture.

1. *Individuality.* Americans are taught that they are separate persons responsible for their own stations in life and in command of their own destiny. They are independent, self-reliant, not tied to their mother's apron strings.
2. *Freedom.* They value the right to exercise choice in all things, move wherever they choose, and are immune from arbitrary exercise of authority. Personal privacy is their right.
3. *Equality.* Americans want to be treated as equals without discrimination because of race, creed, age, sexual preference, status in life.
4. *Democracy.* They support a government by, for, and of the people as the source of political authority. The majority rule.
5. *Humanitarianism.* Americans feel morally obligated to support improved living conditions and the personal welfare of all humanity.
6. *Progress.* They are receptive to change and stress the future. They are motivated to achieve.
7. *Activism.* Action is prized among Americans. They like to be involved doing things, not sitting around talking.
8. *Achievement.* They respect high achievers, self-made persons, and those who succeed.
9. *Practicality.* Americans are governed by what is pragmatic, possible, and attainable. They emphasize efficiency and stress competency.
10. *Time.* Time is money to Americans. They like to get to the point quickly and not "beat around the bush." They are direct and assertive.
11. *Informality.* In speech, dress and posture, Americans tend to be casual and relaxed. They address each other by their given names, appear nonchalant, avoid ceremony, and dress casually.
12. *Morality.* Americans tend to judge people on the basis of what is right or wrong, good or bad, proper or improper, ethical or unethical. They are guided by the Christian Bible's Ten Commandments.

These values serve as guides, as directing principles or standards of behavior that motivate one's life. They represent personal codes of conduct and serve as a basis for reasoning or action along with other, more personal values.

*Chapter Fourteen*

# Conclusion

The text, Reflections in Communication: Making Common is basic in orienting students to discuss several principles and concepts of speech communication and is readable and engaging with applications to real-life experiences.

Readers will discover an academic study of communication grounded in interdisciplinary and experiential approaches.

Topics discussed in Chapter 1 include the three views of human nature, with a discussion of the behaviorist, psychoanalytic and humanistic views with activities.

The definition of communication as process, systemic, symbolic and meaning formation is discussed. The values of communication, personal relationship and professional impact are discussed. The models of communication—linear, interactive and transactional—are assessed in relation to communication outcomes. Characteristics of communication are also analyzed.

The chapter on perception includes a definition and relating perception to communication. The chapter also discusses factors that affect reception of stimuli, perceiving and understanding, social perceptions and offers suggestions for improving perception and communication with activities.

The chapter on self-concept includes defining self-concept, development of self-concept, communication and self-concept and activities.

The chapter on language discusses features of symbols, principles of verbal communication, language and meaning, the language paradigm, distinguishing fact from inference, the relationship between language and perception with activities that include a discussion of diverse language functions.

The chapter on non verbal communication deals with assumptions and overview, types and forms of non verbal communication, with activities.

The chapter on listening involves a definition and overview, a questionnaire, a discussion of benefits, roadblocks and forms of non listening, skills that encourage communication with activities on feelings.

The chapter on interviewing includes definitions, situations, types, unlawful questions and communication in an interview.

The chapter on interpersonal communication includes a definition, goal of dyadic communication, a discussion of sensitivity and self-disclosure, assertive communication, theories of relational communication, attraction, how we develop and maintain relationships and activity on increasing intimacy.

The chapter on culture defines intercultural communication, discusses how cultures differ, cultural identity formation and characteristics, an analysis of the relationship between culture and communication and includes activities such as: value statements, assumptions, social change and cultural resume.

The chapter on small groups: concepts and characteristics discusses theoretical definitions, importance and need for groups, the systems perspectives, development of small groups, helping roles, reflective problem solving, with activities.

The chapter on public communications encourages studying public speaking, speaking to inform, communication apprehension, audience analysis, speaking to persuade, with activities.

The chapter on freedom of speech gives an overview, history, democratic values, legal issues for the public speaker, communication and ethics, and dominant US values.

# References

Adler, A. (1958). *Individual psychology of Alfred Adler: A systematic presentation in selections from his writings.* (Anasbacher H. L. & R. I. Anasbacher eds.) New York; Harpercollins.

Adler, A. (1998). *Understanding human nature.* New York: Health Communications, Inc.

Aristotle, *Rhetoric* New York: Appleton-Century Crofts.

Berger, C. R. (1979). Beyond initial interaction: Uncertainty, understanding and the development of interpersonal relationships in H. Giles & R. St. Clair (Eds.), *Language and social psychology.* 122–144 Oxford: Basil Blackwell.

Berger, C. R., & Calabrese, R. J. (1975). Some explorations in initial interaction and beyond: Toward a developmental theory of interpersonal communication. *Human Communication Research, I,* 99–112.

Berger, C. R. & Gudykunst, W. B. (1991). Uncertainty and communication. In B. Dervin & M. Voight (Eds), *Progress in communication sciences.* Norwood, NJ: Ablex.

Berra, Y. (1998). *The Yogi book: I really didn't say everything I said!".* New York: Workman Publishers.

Bierce, A (1966). *The collected writings of Ambrose Bierce.* (3rd ed.). New York: Citadel.

Bormann, E. (1990). *Small group communication: Theory and practice.* Reading, MA: Addison-Wesley Educational Publishers.

Brilhard, J. (1982). *Effective group discussion.* (4th ed.). Dubuque, IA: W.C. Brown Co. Publishers.

Burgoon, J. K. and Saine, T. K. (1978). *The unspoken dialogue: An introduction to nonverbal communication.* Boston: Houghton Mifflin Company.

Burke, E. (1968). *A philosophical enquiry into the origin of our ideas of the sublime and beautiful.* Notre Dame: University of Notre Dame.

Collier, M. J. and Powell, R. (1990) Ethnicity, instructional communication and classroom Systems. *Communication Quarterly*, 38:334–49.

Covey, S. R. (1989). *The seven habits of highly effective people*. New York: Simon and Schuster.

Cronkhite, G. (1976). *Communication and awareness*. Menlo Park, CA: Cummings.

Darwin, C. (1970). *Expression of emotions in man and animals*. Chicago: University of Chicago Press.

Davis, M. (1975). *Intimate relations*. New York: The Free Press.

DeVito, J.A. (2000). The elements of public speaking. New York: Longman.

Dewey, J. (1971). *How we think*. Chicago: Henry Regenry.

Duck, S. (1991). *Understanding relationships*. New York: Guilford Press.

Emerson, R. W. (2000). *The essential writings of Ralph Waldo Emerson*. (B. Atkinson Ed.). New York: Modern Library.

Emerson, T. I. (1970). The system of freedom of expression. New York: Random House.

Erikson, E. (1994). *Insight and responsibility*. New York: W. W. Norton & Company.

Fine, S. and Penland, P. (1974). *Group dynamics and individual development*. New York: Dekker.

Freud, S. (1910). *The origin and development of psychoanalysis*. New York: Macmillan Company.

Freud, S. (1916). *Psychopathology of everyday life*. Macmillan Company.

Freud, S. (1927). *The ego and id*. (J. Riviere, Trans.) London: L & Virginia Woolf at the Hogarth press. (Original work published 1923).

Giffin, K. & Patton, B. R. (1971). *Fundamentals of interpersonal communications*. New York: Harper & Row.

Giffin, K. & Patton, B. R. (1978). *Decision-making group interaction*. New York: HarperCollins Publishers.

Goffman, E. (1959). *The presentation of self in everyday life*. New York: Doubleday Publishing.

Gronbeck, B. (1978). The rhetoric of political corruption: Sociolinguistic, dialectical, and ceremonial processes. *Quarterly Journal of Speech*. 64/2: 155–72.

Gunther, B. (1986). *Sense relaxation: With a new experiential introduction*. North Hollywood, CA: Newcastle Publishing.

Hall, E. T. (1959). *The silent language*. Greenwich, CT: Fawcett.

Hambrick, R. S. (1991). *The management skills builder: Self-directed learning strategies for career development*. New York: Praeger.

Harris, T. E. & Sherblom, J. C. (2006). Small groups and team communication, 2nd ed. 124–143. Boston: Allyn and Bacon.

Hudson, R. A. (1980). *Sociolinguistics*. Cambridge: CUP.

Hull, C. L. (1943). *Principles of behavior: An introduction to behavior theory*. New York Appleton-Centry-Crofts.

Hull, C. L. (1951). *Essentials of behavior*. New Haven: Yale University Press.

Jackson, D. D. & Ledererd, W. J. (1968). *The mirages of marriage*. New York: W. W. Norton & Company.

Jung, C. (1976). *The psychological types*. (H. G. Baynes, Trans.). New Jersey: Princeton University Press.

Jung, C. (1980). *The archetypes & the collective unconscious.* (R. F. C. Hull, Trans.). New Jersey: Princeton University Press.

Kloff, D. W. & McCroskey, J. (2007). Intercultural communication encounters. Boston: Pearson.

Knapp, M. L. & Hall, A. J (2002). Elements of nonverbal communication in Nonverbal communication in human interaction. 5th ed. Wadsworth 7–18.

Knobloch, L. K. (2007). Perceptions of turmoil within courtship. *Journal of Social and Personal Relationships* 24(3) 363–384.

Knobloch, L. K., Solomon, D. H. & Theiss, J. (2006). The role of intimacy in the production and perception of relationship talk within courtship. *Communication Research* 33/4 Aug 211–25.

Kockelman, P. (2006). Representation of the world: Memories, perceptions, beliefs, intentions and plans. *Semiotics* 162(1) 73–125.

Korzybski, A. (1995). *Science and sanity: An introduction to Non-Aristotelian systems and general semantics* Englewood, NJ: Institute of General Semantics.

Larossa, R. & Reitzes, D. (1993). Symbolic interaction and family studies. Sourcebook of Family Theories and Methods: A contextual Approach, 135–163. New York: Plenum.

Lumsden, G. & Lumsden, D. (1997) Communicating in groups and teams. Belmont, Calif.: Wadsworth.

Maslow, A. H. (1968). *Toward a psychology of being.* New York: Van Nostrand Reinhold Company.

Maslow, A. (2002). *The psychology of science: A reconnaissance.* Chapel Hill, NC: Maurice Bassett Publishing.

McCroskey, J. & Lawrence (1976) *Introduction to human communication.* Boston: Allyn and Bacon.

McCroskey, J. (1993). *An introduction to rhetorical communication.* Englewood Cliffs, NJ: Prentice Hall.

Mead, G. (1932). *The philosophy of the present.* (A. Murphy., ed.) Chicago: Open Court Place.

Mead, G. (1934). *Mind, self, and society.* Chicago: University of Chicago.

Meharabian, A. (1972). Nonverbal communication. Chicago: Aldine Atherton.

Nilsen, T. R. (1974). Ethics of speech communication. Indianapolis, Ind.: Bobbs-Merrill.

Palazzolo, C. (1981). *Small group: An introduction.* New York: D. Van Nostrand Company.

Porter, R. & Samovar, L. (1982). *Intercultural communication: A reader.* Belmont, CA: Wadsworth Publishing Company.

Schwartz, D. J. (1987). *Magic of thinking success.* North Hollywood, CA: Wilshire Book Company.

Shaw, C. M. & Edward, R. (1997). Self-concept and self-presentation of males and females: Similarities and differences. *Communication Reports.* 10/1 Winter, 55–62.

Skinner, B. F. (1948). *Walden two.* New York: Macmillan Publishing Co., Inc.

Skinner, B. F. (1953). *Science and human behavior.* New York: Macmillan Free Press.

Skinner, B. F. (1974). *About behaviorism.* New York: Macmillan Free Press.

Slater, P. (1972). *The pursuit of loneliness: American culture at the breaking point.* Boston: Beacon Press.

Steiner, I (1972). *Group process & productivity.* New York: Academic Press.

Taylor, A. (1988). *Woman communicating.* B. Dervin (Ed.). Norwood, NJ: Ablex.

Tedford, T. L. (1985). Freedom of speech in the United States. New York: Random House.

Viscott, D. (1988). *Risking.* New York: Macmillan Publishers.

Watson, J. (1919). *Psychology: From the standpoint of a behaviorist.* Philadelphia: J. B. Lippincott Company.

Watson, J. (1970). *Behviorism.* New York: W. W. Norton & Company.

Weaver, R. (1967). *Ideas have consequences.* Chicago: University of Chicago Press.

Weaver, R. (1968). *The ethics of rhetoric.* Chicago: Renery Publishing.

Wood, J. T. (2001). *Communication mosaics: An introduction to the field of communication.* (2nd ed.). Belmont, CA: Thomson Learning Inc.

Zorn, T. E. (1998). Educating professional communicators: Limited options in the new academic marketplace. *Australian Journal of Communication,* 25.

# Index